MW00711252

Preliminary Report On The Geology Of Ulster County

James Hall

In the interest of creating a more extensive selection of rare historical book reprints, we have chosen to reproduce this title even though it may possibly have occasional imperfections such as missing and blurred pages, missing text, poor pictures, markings, dark backgrounds and other reproduction issues beyond our control. Because this work is culturally important, we have made it available as a part of our commitment to protecting, preserving and promoting the world's literature. Thank you for your understanding.

GEOLOGICAL SURVEY OF THE STATE OF NEW YORK.
(GEOLOGICAL MAP.)

PRELIMINARY REPORT

ON THE

GEOLOGY OF ULSTER COUNTY.

JAMES HALL, State Geologist.   N. H. DARTON, Assistant.

1892-1893.

PLATE 1.

Overlook Mountain and Front of Northern Catskills. From West Hurley, Looking North. (In the Text of this Paper, the Author Specifies as Plate 1, a Stereogramic Map of Ulster County, but no such Map was Furnished with the Report, and the above View was Found with this Numbering.)

U of M

029 up1ctu

GEOLOGICAL SURVEY OF THE STATE OF NEW YORK.
(GEOLOGICAL MAP.)

Preliminary Report on the Geology of Ulster County.

BY N. H. DARTON.

CONTENTS:

JAMES HALL, *State Geologist:*

SIR.— Ulster county is in central southeastern New York and occupies an area of approximately 1400 square miles.

It extends from a frontage along the Hudson river about thirty-seven miles westward into the southern Catskills. To the south it is bounded by Orange county, to the southwest by Sullivan county, to the northwest by Delaware county, and to the north by Greene county.

The area of Ulster county presents a considerable diversity of topographic features, comprising mountains of several kinds, hills and ridges in great variety, valleys of a number of types, terraces, glacial phenomena and drainage in various stages of development.

In plate 1 an attempt has been made to represent the principal physiographic features of the county by a device known as a

OMITTED

Ref. M.R. 5-4-39

stereogramic map. The stereographic lines of which this map is constructed, define profiles drawn at such frequent intervals that with some additional shading they give a pictorial effect.

The western portion of the county is occupied by the southern portion of the Catskill mountains, which cover about half of its area. From the foot of the Catskill mountains there is a region of high plateaus which extend eastward for some distance and terminate in a steep descent to a valley occupied in greater part by portions of the Rondout and Esopus creeks. East of this valley there is a series of ridges of greater or less height which expand and rise into the Shawangunk* mountain southward. These ridges are parallel to the Hudson north of Kingston and separated from the river bank by a terrace of moderate height. The Shawangunk mountain extends to the southward across the southern half of the county and is separated from the Hudson valley by the wide valley of the Wallkill and a series of narrow ridges extending from south of Rondout to west of Marlborough. Between these ridges and the river there is a high undulating terrace which terminates in steep slopes or rocky faces along the river shore.

The Catskill mountains are a complex of ridges becoming very high, rounded or terraced summits. These summits are separated by depressions of various sizes and the ridges are separated by deep valleys, of which many head in relatively low divides. Originally the region was a plain and there may be minute remnants of this plain on some of the higher summits, but else-where it has been removed by erosion, and the present surface of the region consists entirely of long, steep slopes.

The greater part of the Catskill mountains in Ulster county is confined to the southern Catskills or Shandaken ranges, which are separated from the northern Catskills by the deep, wide valley of Esopus creek. In the northern townships there are Overlook and Rose mountains and some of the lower ridges lying on the slopes of the northern Catskills. The altitudes of the principal high summits are given in the following table, which is taken from Guyot's memoir.†

---

* The pronunciation of this Indian name is *Shongum*, according to local usage.

† Physical structure and hypsometry of the Catskill mountains, Am. Jour. Sci., 3d series, vol. 19, pp. 429-451.

	Feet.		Feet.
Slide mountain	4205	Panther mountain	3828
Peak-o-moose	3875	Spruce top	3567
Table mountain	3865	Eagle mountain	3560
Graham mountain	3886	Balsam mountain	3601
Double top	3875	Belle Ayre mountain	3394
Lone mountain	3680	Overlook mountain	3150
Mt. Cornell	3881	High Point	3100
Wittemberg mountain	3778		

The larger valleys of the Catskills are those of the Esopus creek and the lower portions of some of its branches, Rondout creek, the branches of the Neversink and Dry brook. They are deep and steep sided but contain flats of greater or less width at the bottom. The slopes consist of alternations of irregular rocky ledges usually in more or less continuous terraces, with intermediate slopes of varying degrees of steepness. The low divides at the heads of the principal streams and certain of their branches are very remarkable features of physiography of the Catskills and their origin is not entirely clear. They are air gaps having a depth of nearly 2000 feet in the case of Stony Clove and they afford the principal means of communication through the ranges. The divide in Stony Clove is 2100* feet above tide level; the gap at Pone hill, 1886 feet; Mount Hollow, 2650* feet; divide between Big Indian and East Branch of Neversink, 2700† feet; West Branch of Neversink-Beaverkill divide, 2650† feet; Peak-o-moose gap at head of Rondout creek, 1640† feet; Kaaterskill-Schoharie creek divide, 1925* feet; Plattekill-Schoharie divide, 1925* feet, and there may be others which are more or less distinctly indicated in plate 1. Stony Clove, " Peak-o-moose " gap, Mink Hollow and Deep Hollow gaps are very narrow rocky gorges with walls rising steeply 1200 feet or more, and long steep slopes above to the level of the adjoining summits. The others are wide depressions with slopes of various degrees of steepness. Excepting in the Plattekill and Kaaterskill divides the slopes are from the center of the gaps and about the same in degree in either direction. The Plattekill and Kaaterskill have cut deep gorges in the steep eastern slope of the northern Catskills which head in

---

* U. S. Geol. Survey determinations.
† Aneroid determinations by N. H. Darton. The others are from Guyot.

the wide gently west sloping valley of the two head branches of the Schoharie creek. They present an unsurpassed illustration of stream-robbing, for they have cut off the upper waters of these Schoharie branches and carry them directly to the Hudson. This is also the case with the Sawkill in the center of Woodstock township, where it has tapped the headwaters of the Beaverkill over falls into a gorge with walls 800 to 900 feet in height.

The steep eastern front of the Catskill mountains is one of their most notable features and it adds greatly to their prominence. In the northern Catskills the front rises abruptly from 1500 to 2500 feet out of a plain of which the average altitude is about 450 feet above tide level. It is a relatively even slope comprising a great succession of steep, narrow terrace scarps which are broken only by the Kaaterskill and Plattekill gorges. In the southern Catskills the front has a similar abruptness but its slope is broken by long spurs. ·

The belt lying east of the Catskills is a high plateau with its surface broken by low, wide terraces and it is crossed by the streams in deep rocky gorges. It is terminated eastward by very steep slopes which extend across the country from northeast to southwest as a prominent escarpment. The valley at its foot is continuous across the county and is occupied in greater part by the middle portion of the Rondout creek and lower Esopus creek. The ridges eastward are a succession of long north and south trending ranges of moderate height. The eastward range presents a limestone cliff of greater or less elevation to the eastward through the greater part of its course. These ranges expand and rise into the Shawangunk mountain north of Rosendale, and this mountain is a prominent feature in the south-central townships. In its broader portion it comprises several ridges and attains an elevation of over 2200 feet. It has a slope westward to the Rondout valley and presents to the eastward a vertical escarpment of conglomerate surmounting long slopes of shales. It narrows greatly near the southern border of the county, and extends far to the southward as a narrow single-crested ridge with long western slope and an east-facing escarpment at the west of its eastern slopes.

The Wallkill valley region comprises broad belts of level or gently-rolling lands along the Wallkill, Swartzkill and Plattekill and rounded hills of moderate elevation on the adjacent slopes. Along the base of the Shawangunk mountain these hills increase considerably in altitude, but their rounded form is unchanged.

East of the Wallkill valley there rises the series of high ridges which constitute Marlborough mountain and its northern continuation to Hussy hill south of Rondout. They present considerable diversity in topography, but are mainly rocky and very steep sided. The higher ridges average about 1000 feet in altitude, but there are many irregularities in their course as shown in the stereogram. The deepest depressions across the range are west of Highland and Ulster Park stations.

GENERAL STRUCTURE.

The general structural relations of Ulster county are represented in sections of figure 1.

The rocks are a series of widely extended sheets of sandstone, shales, limestone and conglomerates. The uppermost or youngest member is on the higher summits of the Catskill mountains, and the lowest or oldest which appears on the surface, is a limestone which occupies a very small area in the southeastern corner of the county.

In the Catskill mountains and their foothills there are several thousand feet of sandstones and shales which are overlaid in the higher regions by conglomeratic sandstones. These beds all dip gently to the west-southwest, possibly with slight undulations. In the lower lands and ridges east of the Catskill mountains there is a succession of limestones and shales which to the southward are underlaid by a sheet of hard conglomerate which gives rise to Shawangunk mountain. In this belt the gentle westerly dip gradually gives place to flexures, some of which are of considerable steepness. The limestone series and Shawangunk conglomerate are underlaid unconformably by the shales and sandstones of the Hudson river formations which extend to the Hudson river. In the southeastern portion of the county the beds are steeply overturned and inclined mainly to the eastward.

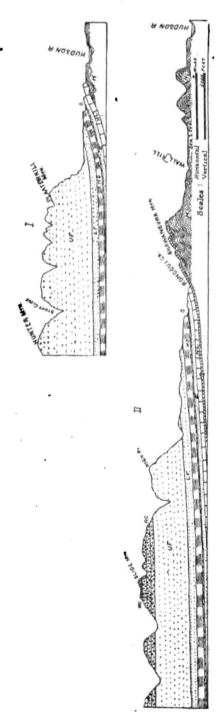

FIG. 1.—Cross sections of Ulster county. I. Through Saugerties township. II. Through Slide mountain near Highlands, looking north. WC., White conglomerate sandstone; RC., Red conglomerate sandstone; UF., Upper Flag series; LF., Lower Flag series; HS., Hamilton shales; O., Onondaga limestone; E., Esopus shales and Oriskany sandstone; HL., Helderberg limestone and Salina waterlime series, and including Niagara limestone on I and Clinton and Medina sandstone and shales on II; S., Shawangunk grit; H., Hudson river shales; Hs., Hudson river sandstones.

Along the river terraces and in the larger valleys there are extensive areas of clay and sands, and in nearly every part of the county there are accumulations of drift gravels and sands of greater or less extent.

STRATIGRAPHY.

The rocks of Ulster county comprise formations from lower Silurian to upper Devonian age lying in two comformable successions separated by an unconformity at the top of the lower Silurian. These members, with their ages, thickness and general characteristics, are listed in their regular succession in the following table :

NAMES.	Age.	Character.	Thickness
....	Catskill..........	White conglomeratic sandstones.......	850+
	Chemung........	Red conglomeratic sandstones.........	1875+
Upper Flag series......	Oneonta (Portage)..........	Gray sandstones and flags, with red shales	3000+ 500
Lower Flag series.....	Hamilton.....	Gray sandstones and flags, with black shales	600
Hamilton shales........		Black shales, with thin sandstones.....	
Onondaga limestone	Onondaga......	Gray cherty limestone	60
Esopus shales	Caudi-galli' grit.	Black slaty shales.....................	200-300
Oriskany sandstone	Oriskany	Calcareous sandstones and conglomerate	5-40
Upper shaly limestone		Impure limestone	80-125
Becraft limestone		Limestone............................	20-80
Lower shaly limestone	Helderberg....	Impure limestone	60
Pentamerus limestone.		Dark massive limestones..............	80-60
Tentaculite limestone..		Thin-bedded limestones...............	20-40
Cement series	Salina	Cement and waterlime	20-50
Niagara limestone	Niagara	Coralline limestone	0-8
Clinton and Medina	Clinton-Medina.	Red shales, sandstones and quartzites.	0-45
Shawangunk grit........	Oneida	Conglomerate	0-250
Hudson River formation	Hudson River ..	Black shales and sandstone............	1800+
Wappinger limestone ...	Calciferous	Limestone............................	200+

White conglomeratic sandstone.—This formation caps Slide mountain and the summits of some adjacent peaks. It is a coarse-grained, heavily-bedded, moderately-hard sandstone containing disseminated pebbles and conglomeratic streaks. The pebbles are of quartz and quartzite in greater part, of light color and small size. Its greatest thickness is seen on Slide mountain, where there are 350 feet; the outliers or adjacent summits are very much less in thickness. The colors are in greater part very light gray, but some portions are greenish or brownish, particularly toward the base of the formation. There are several intercalated beds of somewhat finer-grained sandstones. The pebbles and conglomeratic streaks are of very irregular occurrence, but they exist in appreciable proportion in nearly every bed.

It is not, by any means, the highest formation in the Catskill mountains, and is probably a local development. This formation, and the underlying members to the base of the Upper Flag series, belong to the Catskill group of Mather and Vanuxem.

Red conglomeratic sandstones.— This member occupies the higher portions of the western townships. It consists of coarse, heavily-bedded sandstones of dull brownish hue, containing dis seminated pebbles and conglomeratic streaks and only differs from the overlying white conglomeratic beds in its color. It should not be classed as a conglomerate for the reason that it is in greater part composed of sand grains. The pebbles and conglomeratic portions are scattered very irregularly through the series, but are nearly everywhere more or less conspicuous. The bedding is thinner and flaggy at some portions, and there is much coarser cross bedding. Locally there are included masses of more or less heavily-bedded gray sandstone, but these are of no great thickness, and are not conspicuous features. Several thin layers of red shales also occur. This series merges into the underlying Upper Flag series by a short, irregular transition which may vary somewhat in horizon. The thickness of the beds in Ulster county is about 1375 feet to the eastward and apparently somewhat more to the westward. The formation constitutes the higher slope of the Slide mountain ridge and all of the higher region west of the heads of Big Indian and Neversink creeks.

The Upper Flagstone series.— This formation consists of a thickness of thin and thick-bedded sandstones with intercalated red shales, occupying a wide area in the middle and lower portions of the Catskill mountains. The red shale intercalations are thickest and most frequent to the northwestward and in the lower members. Above and to the west and south they occur less frequently and in thinner beds. The sandstones occur in series from 20 to 200 feet in thickness, which give rise to sharp terraces in the northern slopes. They are in greater part light-gray to gray-brown in color and from two to six inches in thickness. Many of the beds are suitable for flagging or for "bluestone," and these are worked at numerous localities in the upper valleys of Esopus creek, and along the eastern slopes of the Catskills. Portions of the sandstones are in heavy masses with cross-bedded structure, and these members are usually of exceptional hardness. There are in this series occasional intercalations of dark-colored shales, but they are very infrequent, and I have not observed any of greater thickness than three feet. There are also local occurrences of conglomerated sandstone and scattered pebbles, some beds of which occur at two horizons on Overlook mountain. The red shales occur in beds varying from a few inches to thirty feet, but are usually not over ten feet. They are most frequent and extensive in Woodstock and adjacent townships. In the western part of the county there are red shales at long intervals among the upper members of the formation. In Wawarsing and Rochester townships there are several beds of red shales in the lower members. The thickness of the formation is about 3000 feet, but the precise amount can be determined only by careful, instrumental measurements. The members of the formation are nearly everywhere exposed within its area, particularly the harder sandstones, which give rise to cliffs of greater or less prominence. The finest successions of outcrops are in the valley of the Esopus creek, the upper valley of Rondout creek, the west branch of Neversink, the Rondout valley below Lackawack, and along the slopes of the northern Catskills in Woodstock township and west of Saugerties.

Lower flagstone series.— This series consists of beds of thin-bedded sandstones with intercalated beds of dark shales. It extends diagonally across the county from Saugerties to Wawarsing townships and constitutes a range of hills and terraces lying next east from the foothills of the Catskills. It is the principal source of the great bluestone product of Ulster county, and it contains a number of heavy beds of this material.

Sandstones constitute the larger portion of the series, and they give rise to terraces of greater or less width and height in the less disturbed portion of the region. They are in masses which vary from a few inches to forty feet in thickness but in greater part average from ten to fifteen feet. The color varies from greenish-gray to light bluish-gray but some portions are dark gray. The rock is mostly moderately fine grained, but the grain varies somewhat. The texture is porous and the hardness is high. The beds of which the masses are constituted vary from half an inch to a foot in thickness, the same bed often presenting considerable variability in this regard. The intercalated shales are in beds from a few inches to eight or ten feet in thickness. Their color is dark gray to black in greater part, but some portions are brownish or greenish. Among the upper members of the series there are several thin, discontinuous streaks of light greenish and reddish shales interbedded among the dark shales and constituting beds of passage to the overlying Upper Flag series.

Thin streaks of quartz conglomerate were noticed at several localities interbedded among the flags, notably in the lower beds of the Jocky Hill region

The flag beds are exposed over wide areas in the quarry districts of Saugerties, Kingston, Hurley and Marbletown townships where they dip gently to the westward. The heavy masses give rise to terraces separated by slopes of shale or the thinner-bedded, softer sandstones. In southern Rochester and Wawarsing townships the beds are tilted steeply to the westward and their outcrop belt is greatly narrowed. In this region their upturned edges give rise to a high, rough range of hills lying between the foot of the Catskills and the Rondout-Sandburg valley.

The thickness of the Upper Flag series is about 500 feet, but no careful measurement was made.

The age of the series is not definitely known, but it is in the main of the upper Hamilton group; the shales and some of the sandstone beds contain fossils, but these have not yet been studied.

Hamilton shales. — This formation consists of a series of dark-gray to black or brown shales containing thin sandy beds, particularly in its upper part. It constitutes the steep slopes rising from the wide valley of Onondaga limestone to the terraces and plateaus of the Lower Flag series. In Wawarsing township, where the beds are steeply tilted, all but its uppermost members are deeply eroded and underlie the western side of the Sandburg Creek valley. In Mount Marion southwest of Saugerties the formation attains its greatest prominence, rising in a steep face high above the limestone region eastward. The beds are nearly everywhere exposed excepting the basal members which usually underlie the western edges of the valley at the face of the slope. The immediately overlying beds give rise to frequent cliffs of moderate height, and in these there were seen alternations of harder and softer dark-colored shales with thin sandy intercala-tions.

The upper beds are harder and contain scattered flaggy layers capping the slopes and constituting terraces along them. The summit of the formation has been considered at the base of the heavy flag belts of the Lower Flag series, but this may vary somewhat in horizon through the length of the county. The thickness averages about 600 feet. The beds are of the age of the lower Hamilton group, but the precise equivalence is not known. Fossils occur sparingly throughout the series, but they have not as yet been systematically collected or studied.

Onondaga limestone.—The occurrence of this formation is of considerable economic importance, for it furnishes lime of excellent quality which has been burnt at many localities. It is also a source of building stone not only for local use but for the market. The formation is a light bluish-gray limestone, dense in texture, and in greater part massively bedded. It contains much chert mainly in thin beds and elongated lenses, but this is sometimes absent locally. The chert predominates in the upper beds, but it is also usually present in the lower beds. The basal layers of the Onondaga limestones are beds of passage from the preceding formation, and for several feet in thickness consist of intermixtures of clayey and sandy rocks which gradually emerge upward into the fine limestone. The top of the formation is rarely exposed and I found no outcrop in Ulster county owing to the drift filled valley which here always occupies the Onondaga-Hamilton boundary belt.

The outcrop of the Onondaga limestone is practically continuous from the northeastern corner of the county to Wawarsing township, through which outcrops are rarely observed. For the greater part of its course it dips west into the wide valley, across which rise the steep slopes of the Hamilton ridge.

About Kingston the outcrop of the formation widens greatly in the series of gentle folds which traverse the region and

most of the upper part of the city is built upon its area.
Southward by Hurley and Marbletown the formation is a conspicuous feature in the ridge sloping west to Esopus creek.
Farther south its outcrops are widely scattered. North from
Kingston there are extensive exposures along the West Shore
railroad and for a short distance east nearly to Saugerties where
the railroad turns off to the northeast. From west of Saugerties
to Asbury, exposures are very conspicuous along and near the
road passing through Cedar Grove and Katsbaan. The thickness
of the formation is at least sixty feet in Ulster county and does
not appear to vary in amount.

Cauda-galli grit=Esopus slate.— This is, in greater part, a hard
gritty shale giving rise to ridges, not unusually of large size but
characterized by sharp contour and generally occurring in considerable number across the breadth of the outcrop of the formation. The slate is dark in color, often pitch black when fresh,
brittle but tough in texture and massively bedded. The bedding
is seldom conspicuous, for the formation is traversed by a slaty
cleavage which crosses the bedding plane at high angles and
along which the material readily cleaves into slaty fragments.
The bedding planes are not lines of ready separation. Where the
surface of the bedding planes are exposed they usually present
impressions of a characteristic fossil which gave the original name
"Caudi-galli grit" to the formation. This, as its name implies, has
the form of a cock's tail in general outline and is supposed to be
due to a fucoid which has been named *Spirophyton caudi-galli.*
The upper member of the formation merges into the Onondaga
limestone as described above, but it is sharply separated from the
underlying formation by an abrupt change in the character of
materials. The finest exposures are in the hills south and east of
Kingston and along Esopus creek above Saugerties. The nature
of the latter is shown in plate 3.

Its extent is about the same as that of the Onondaga limestone
or slightly greater, and its outcrop is along a parallel belt lying
next east. It often constitutes the crest of the ridge with the
Onondaga limestone lying on the slope westward. Its soil is
usually very thin and barren. In Rochester and Wawarsing
townships its upper members become harder and less broken by

slaty cleavage This is notably the case at the falls caused by it a mile northeast of Pattankunk.

From Wawarsing township southward the rock is not exposed, so far as I know, but it underlies the Sandburg Creek valley.

The thickness in the northern part of the county is about 200 feet; about Kingston it is fully 300 feet, but southward it probably thins somewhat although beyond Rosendale I could find no complete sections from which an estimate of thickness could be made.

The Oriskany sandstone.—This thin but characteristic formation lies immediately beneath the Esopus shales, either at the base of the first Esopus shale ridge or constituting a narrow ridge just east or south. It appears to be continuous throughout Ulster county but in some regions is hidden by drift or debris. It presents a variety of components in this region, some of which were not observed elsewhere. In greater part it is a very silicious limestone, but about Rondout and Wilbur it contains a bed of small pebble conglomerate to which attention has been called by Davis.* The thickness of the formation is very variable. West of Saugerties, seven feet of quartzitic beds are seen; along Esopus creek there are twelve feet of calcareous beds, and at Rondout, thirty feet, including the conglomeratic member. In the Whiteport region and southward the formation consists of a silicious limestone bed which has a thickness of from eight to nine feet. Near Wawarsing the thickness is ten to fifteen feet. The formation is very fossiliferous throughout; the casts and impressions of the shells appearing prominently in the weathered surface of the beds. The most notable occurrence of fossils is along the east bank of Esopus creek below Glenerie, where they abound. They are also abundant at some points about Rondout and along the Wallkill Valley railroad, north of Whiteport.

Upper Shaly limestone.—This is the upper member of the lower Helderberg limestone formation.

The upper Shaly beds are very impure limestones containing a considerable proportion of clay and sand. They are somewhat massively bedded, but their most prominent physical feature is their slaty cleavage. Owing to their hardness

---

* Nonconformity at Rondout. Am. Jour. Science, III, vol. 26, page 392.

and the cleavage they give rise to small, very rough ridges similar to those of Esopus shale, but usually of even rougher surface.   In some regions they constitute the steep eastern face of a ridge of which the crest and western slope are Oriskany sandstone.   Notwithstanding the slaty cleavage the beds are everywhere fossiliferous but the remains are often much distorted. The thickness of this member is about 125 feet in the central and southern portion of the county, decreasing gradually in the Saugerties region to from thirty to thirty-five feet, near the Greene county line.   The upper Shaly limestone appears to merge into the Oriskany beds at some localities, but it is quite abruptly separated from the Becraft beds below.

The Becraft limestone.— These are thick beds of a relatively pure, light bluish-gray to pinkish-gray limestone of semi-crystalline grain, and made up in considerable portion of shell and shell fragments.   Among these fragments there are characteristic saucer-shaped masses of white crystallized carbonate of lime mostly from an inch to two inches in diameter representing the bases of the heads of crinoids.   These were regarded as Scutellæ [from their form only] by some of the earlier observers, and their conspicuous occurrence in this member gave the original name of " Scutella limestone."   The thickness of the formation averages from twenty to thirty feet.   It is quite extensively worked for lime burning near Rondout and Whiteport and affords excellent lime.   In plate 5 there are shown some of its features in a quarry near Rondout.

The Becraft limestone extends in a narrow but continuous band entirely through the eastern part of the county.   Its most prominent exposures are between Saugerties and Rondout, and about Wilbur and Whiteport.   It is rarely seen to the southwestward where an outcrop at Millhook and another a mile southwest of High Falls are the principal exposures.

Lower Shaly limestone.— This formation is precisely similar to the upper Shaly beds and the two members·are co-extensive in Ulster county.   The thickness averages from sixty to seventy feet throughout.   The very rough little ridges to which this formation gives rise are particularly conspicuous in the Binnewater region where they are repeated by many small folds and are very steep and craggy.   The beds are extensively exposed about Wilbur and Rondout and along the crest of the limestone ridge extending from Rondout to Saugerties.

Pentamerus limestone.— This member is a hard, dark blue or lead colored, somewhat cherty, massively-bedded limestone, which gives rise to conspicuous cliffs throughout the greater part of its outcrop. These cliffs are due mainly to the toughness and massiveness of the beds together with a disposition to vertical jointing, and the presence of underlying beds of much softer texture. Another characteristic feature is a sub-bedding along irregular waving lines which are brought out by weathering. The limestone is sparingly fossiliferous, containing principally the characteristic *Pentamerus galeatus* which was seen in all localities.

The most prominent exposures are the cliffs at Rosendale and northward, about Port Jackson, near Eddyville and along the eastern face of the limestone ridge extending from Rondout to Saugerties and West Camp. These cliffs vary in height, but are usually continuous for long distance. Two miles north of Rondout they approach to within a few yards of the shore of the Hudson but to the northward they trend farther back and are separated from the river banks by a terrace averaging somewhat over a mile in width. In the widely corrugated region about Rosendale, Whiteport and the Binnewater, the exposures are extensive. Along the axis of the principal anticlinal in this region, the beds rise in high ridges for some distance.

The thickness of the Pentamerus limestone is variable. About Kingston and northward it is from thirty to forty feet. About Whiteport the same, and at Rosendale considerably more, attaining a maximum of sixty feet. To the southwestward its full thickness is not exhibited.

Tentaculite limestone.— This is in greater part a thin-bedded, dark-blue limestone constituting the basal members of the Helderberg limestones. The beds are for the most part from two to three inches thick and they separate along smooth bedding planes. The formation has a thickness of from twenty to forty feet, its greatest development being in the vicinity of Rosendale and Rondout. There is included at or near its base, notably in the quarries near Rondout, a dark-gray, impure limestone containing many corals and representing the Stromatopora horizon. The Tentaculite beds appear to be continuous throughout, but they are usually

hidden by the talus from the Pentamerus cliffs above, and outcrops are rare. They are well exposed in the cement quarries at
Rosendale, Whiteport, East Kingston and Rondout, and also
near West Camp.

The Salina waterlime beds.—These members are a southeastern
extension of the Salina formation of central New York, and the
cement beds which they here carry are the most important mineral
resource of Ulster county. The usual characters of the formation
are thin-bedded water limestones and the cement is of local occurrence. It is a blue black, very fine grained, massively-bedded
deposit, consisting of calcareous, magnesian and argillaceous
materials in somewhat variable proportions. The beds are
extensively developed in the Rondout and Rosendale regions.
They come in gradually and are attended by a thickening of the
formation from its usual average of twenty to thirty feet to forty
or fifty feet. At Rondout the principal cement bed has a thickness averaging about twenty feet. It lies directly on the coralline
(Niagara) limestone and is overlaid by alternating successions of
waterlime and thin impure cement beds. The cement horizon is
not exposed far north of East Kingston, but how far it extends
to the northward is not known. It is seen to thicken southward
and it attains its maximum thickness in the vicinity of Rondout,
thinning out again and giving place to waterlime beds south of
Wilbur. It is seen to have come in again in the Whiteport
anticlinal, which brings up a great development of cement beds
along its principal axis from Whiteport to Rosendale. Some
features of the beds in this region are shown in the plates. They
also come out along the eastern limb of the synclinal eastward.
To the south of Rosendale the cement beds continue up the Coxingkill valley and around the point of the anticlinal by High Falls
on the Rondout creek. Above this place it can be traced but a
short distance owing to its deep erosion and heavy drift cover in
the Rondout Creek valley, but its reappearance near Port Jackson
indicates that it probably continues for a considerable distance.

In the Whiteport–Rosendale region there are two beds of
cement, the lower averaging twenty-one feet in thickness, and
the other averaging twelve feet in thickness with an intervening member of ten to fifteen feet of waterlime beds, but these

amounts vary considerably. At High Falls the upper bed is fifteen feet thick, the lower bed five feet thick with three feet of intervening waterlime beds. The High Falls are over the thicker bed as is shown in the plates. Cement may be looked for in the upper Rondout valley, from Port Jackson by Ellenville, but owing to absence of outcrops this should only be regarded as a suggestion.

The Coralline limestone (Niagara limestone).—This is a thin bed of dark-gray limestone which underlies the cement at Rondout and for a short distance northward. · In the Rondout quarries its thickness is about seven feet. At the entrance to the quarries in Becraft limestone, a mile north of East Kingston, it is seen to have thinned to five inches. To the northward there are no exposures of this horizon except near the railroad north of West Camp station, where the member is seen with the thickness of three feet. South of· Rondout, in the Whiteport and Rosendale regions, it is absent for the cement is seen lying directly on the surface of sandstones of greater age. The corals in this limestone are of Niagara age, as Dr. James Hall has long ago shown, and this thin bed is the attenuated southeastern extension of the great limestone series which gives rise to the Falls of Niagara.

Clinton and Medina formations.— The beds which are thought to represent these horizons begin a few miles south of Kingston and extend through the Whiteport-Rosendale cement region and up the Rondout Creek valley to Homowack. They present considerable diversity in character. The lower member is red or reddish shale throughout, but the upper beds vary from quartzite northward to shaly and calcareous beds southward.

The formation comes in between the waterlime and Hudson river slates along the base of the ridge, about midway between Wilbur and Eddyville, and thickens gradually to the average of about forty feet in the next five miles. The upper member of white or gray, thin-bedded quartzite begins first and is followed in a couple of miles by an underlying series of hard shales varying in color from dull red to brown. These two members preserve their distinctive characters to some distance beyond Rosendale, where the quartzite gives place to argillaceous and calcareous sediments.

The quartzite is in very regular beds having a thickness from three to twelve inches which are in greater part welded together. The predominating color is light-gray with buff-brown streaks; many of the beds having a characteristic cross-bedding within themselves brought out by slight differences in tints. The lower cement bed lies directly on the surface of this quartzite, but is sharply separated by dissimilarity of materials without beds of passage. The shales underlying the quartzite are in greater part dull-red in color, moderately fine-grained, and massively bedded as a whole, but they readily break into shale on exposure. They are quite sharply separated from the quartzite.

The shales and quartzites are extensively exposed in the cement quarries along the anticlinal of the Rosendale-Whiteport belt and the eastern edge of the synclinal eastward. The two members preserve their distinctive characters to some distance south of Rosendale, where the quartzite gives place to argillaceous and calcareous sediments finely exposed in the north bank of the Rondout, at High Falls. In this region the red of the lower shales increases to a bright tint, which is strikingly exhibited in the High Falls exposure. There are also outcrops of these red beds on the Coxingkill, two miles south-southeast of High Falls, and on the point of an anticlinal near Stony creek, a mile southeast of Port Jackson. Exposures of the members are rare in Wawarsing township, but at several points south of Ellenville there are a few small showings of red and brown shales along the western base of the Shawangunk mountain.

The evidence as to the precise equivalency of these beds between the Shawangunk grit and Salina formation, in Ulster county, is unsatisfactory. No fossils have been found and the physical characters are not wholy distinctive. The quartzite and calcareous upper member is thought to represent the Clinton formation, for the upper part of this horizon is characterized by somewhat similar beds in western New York. The lower red beds may also be Clinton, but as they appear to expand into a series of red sandstones southward, it is suggested that they are of Medina age.

Shawangunk grit.— This formation is a great sheet of silicified quartz conglomerate lying on the Hudson river shales, and giving rise to the Shawangunk mountain. The first appearance of the formation northward is between Binnewater and Whiteport stations, on the Walkill Valley railroad, and in the cement quarries on the eastern side of the ridge eastward, as before noted. In the anticlinal north of Binnewater station, the thickness rapidly increases to sixty feet, but to the eastward it thickens less rapidly and it is discontinuous at several points. Just south of Rosendale it thickens rapidly from east to west to about forty-five feet, and to 100 feet in the ridges which rise to the southwest. About Lake Mohonk fully 160 feet are exposed and at the falls of the Peterkill there are 210 feet in all, but these are localities at which the upper part of the formation has been removed by erosion. The thickness of the formation in the wider part of the mountain is about 200 feet, for on Sam's Point and Millbrook mountain the precipices expose fully this amount. Along the western slope near Ellenville 200 feet seems to be a fair estimate; and the entire thickness is here exposed, but I made no precise measurements.

In greater part the rock consists of white quartz pebbles of small or moderate size in a matrix of sand and silicious cement. Locally there are beds of coarse quartzite or quartzitic sandstones, but the conglomerate is the predominant rock. The color is white, with local exceptions of gray, blue or buff, the latter due mainly to staining from pyrites which is frequently dissemi nated in the rocks. The bedding is predominantly massive, averaging three to four feet, but thinner bedding is sometimes seen particularly in the finer-grained materials. The most conspicuous exposure of thinner bedding is at Awosting or Peterkill falls as shown in an accompanying plate.

The unconformity.— Throughout Ulster county there is unconformity between the upper and lower Silurian sediments, but its amount varies considerably. In the northeastern townships the attenuated eastern representative of the Niagara limestone lies unconformably on the Hudson river shales and the Clinton, Medina and Oneida deposits are absent. South from Rondout the supposed representatives of the Clinton, Medina and Oneida formations come in, in succession, and the Niagara limestone is lacking. In the southern part of the county, where the Shawangunk grit attains great thickness, it lies on an eroded surface of the Hudson river shales throughout. These relations are due to an uplift with erosion at the end of lower Silurian times and probably also to oscillations for a considerable part of the early upper Silurian. Mather and Davis have discussed some of the relations in the Hudson valley, and Dr. James Hall has reviewed the principal features in several papers.

The sequence of events in Ulster county was a general uplift of the deposits at the close of the Hudson river deposition, and erosion of its entire surface. The uplift was attended by considerable folding, the greatest in amount to the northwestward and the flexures were base leveled in some measure. The Oneida, Medina and Clinton appear to have been deposited during subsidence which increased southward so that the deposits overlapped, the latest extending nearly to Kingston. Possibly there was some deposition farther south which was removed by uplifts and erosion of which there is now no evidence. The absence of the Niagara southward, and its thinning north of East Kingston, may be due either to cessation of deposition, or to uplifts of the surface above the waters of Niagara times. With the deposition of the Salina beds there was general subsidence which was long continued.

Hudson river formation.— This formation consists of shales and sandstones. The shales vary from gray-brown to black in color, are fissile, moderately hard for the most part, and give rise to rounded hills which, in the vicinity of Shawangunk mountain, are of considerable height. They contain intercalated beds of sandstone of two kinds, one a very fine-grained, massively bedded, dark-gray or blue-black hard sandstone, of which there are beds occurring widely scattered throughout the formation; and the other, a succession of coarse-grained, dark gray, thin-bedded flaggy sandstones with disseminated pebbles of quartz, slate, and limestone occurring in a series of ridges extending northward through the southeastern corner of the county. The stratigraphy of the formation has not been worked out, and owing to the complicated structure and lack of knowledge of the stratigraphy, the thickness of the formation in Ulster county has not been determined.

PLATE 2.

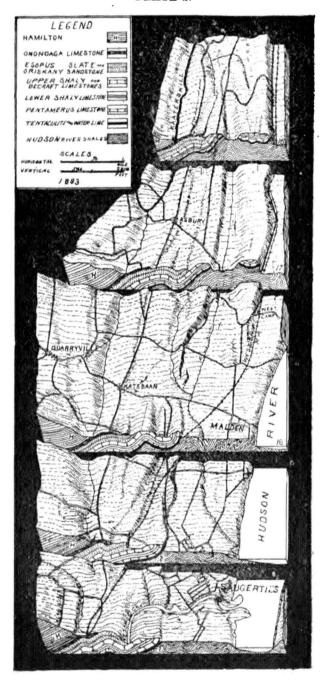

Stereogramic Map and Sections of the Northeastern Part of Saugerties Township.

Wappinger limestone.— This formation occupies a very small area in the southeastern corner of the county, south of Marlborough. It consists of light bluish-gray limestone-containing considerable arenaceous material and closely resembling the purer varieties of the Calciferous sandrock of the Mohawk valley in its general appearance. It has the same dull gray glimmering fracture and similar cavities containing calcite and quartz, and weather to a dull buff tint. The beds are three to four feet thick in greater part, with some shaly streaks showing near the lowest exposures. The thickness above the surface is 150 feet, of which the lower fifty feet outcrop in a cliff along the Hudson river. The formation is the oldest in the county, and its age is upper Cambrian. The beds intervening between the Wappinger limestone and the Hudson river shales are cut out by the fault which has brought the limestone to its present position.

LOCAL GEOLOGY.

The limestone belt from West Camp to Katrine.— In plate 2 there is given a series of cross sections illustrating the principal structural features from several miles above West Camp to a short distance south of Saugerties. The salient features of this portion of the belt are the anticlinal valley and the geosynclinal ridge which end near West Camp, and the anticlinal ridge southeast of Katsbaan. The geosynclinal ridge is considerably eroded near West Camp and contains only a small thickness of lower Shaly beds at the county line. The Pentamerus beds are bared over a considerable area southward and terminate to the east and west in cliffs of considerable prominence. At the base of the cliffs on the east side, just west of the railroad, portions of the Tentaculite and waterlime beds are exposed having an aggregate thickness of about sixty feet. The waterlime beds are not fully exhibited, but there are no traces of cement rock apparent. Underlying them there is exposed at one point a three-foot bed of light blue-gray, tough, massive limestone containing corals of Niagara age. On the west side of the ridge the limestones dip to the west-northwest; on the western side to the east, both at low angles and with a perceptible pitch to the north.

Along the base of the ridge sandstones and shales of Hudson river age are seen with dips essentially the same as those of the overlying limestones. The contact was found. Opposite West Camp station the several limestones end in succession and the elevation of ridge is considerably decreased. It continues for about a mile presenting frequent outdrops of Hudson river shales and fine-grained gray-brown sandstones. Half a mile south of the termination of the limestones the Hudson river beds present a continuation of the synclinal with dips to the eastward of forty degrees to fifty degrees on the west side and a gentle anticlinal on the eastern side.

The anticlinal valley west of the geosynclinal ridge is flat bottomed with many small ridges of Hudson river shales and sandstones occurring at intervals. This valley widens southward and merges into the high terrace level which extends to the bank of the Hudson river. On its west side there are low cliffs of waterlime, Tentaculite and Pentamerus limestone which dip off to the westward, as shown in the section (plate 2). These cliffs have Hudson river slates and sandstones at their base for some distance. But basal contacts were not found here nor for several miles southward, and it is not known whether the coralline (Niagara limestone) is present. Above the crest of this ridge the lower Shaly, Becraft, upper Shaly and Oriskany are more or less widely exposed. On the west side there is a valley mainly in lower beds of the Esopus shales, and this formation extends therein to the road from Asbury to Katsbaan. At Asbury the Onondaga limestones are exposed over a considerable area on the summit and slopes of the ridge sloping to the Beaverkill, beyond which rises the steep slope of the lower Hamilton hills.

The Pentamerus outcrop extends southward to the western part of the village of Saugerties, with the overlying limestones exposed in the crest or on the western slope of the ridge. At a point about a mile and a half south of West Camp station a small fold crosses the belt and gives rise to a noticeable offset in the line of Pentamerus ledges. A short distance south of this there is a depression in which a small stream crosses, and two miles north of Saugerties the ridge is crossed by the West Shore railroad in a low gap with sloping sides. The Esopus shales extend southward in a broad belt which is crossed by the railroad opposite Saugerties. The breadth of this belt is due to two folds of which the anticlinal pitches up for some distance east of Cedar Grove, bringing the Oriskany sandstone, upper Shaly beds and Becraft limestone to the surface in a ridge of some prominence. This ridge is crossed by the upper road from Saugerties to Cedar Grove, on which the formations are well exhibited. The structure of this ridge to the westward is shown in section 18, plate 2. On the section there is a small synclinal tongue of the lower beds on the Onondaga limestone with a narrow strip of the Esopus shales in a valley beyond. This synclinal pitches down to southward and the limestone area extends eastward nearly to Saugerties station. At this station and in the railroad cuts near by, there are excellent exposures of the Esopus shales. They are black, massively bedded and have very distinct cleavage, nearly vertical to the bedding planes. Along the western slope of the ridge east of the station the Oriskany beds outcrop for some distance, and also on the roadside about a mile to the north. They are hard quartzites, eight feet in thickness with a dip to the west of fifty degrees. The underlying Shaly and Becraft limestones outcrop almost continuously in this ridge. Both are highly fossiliferous and very characteristic. There are a number of sharp variations in strike in this vicinity as well as abrupt changes in dip. The lower limestone members on the eastern side of the ridge dip at angles of from twenty degrees to thirty degrees. This dip, which increases to fifty degrees or sixty degrees on the western side of the ridge, soon gives place to gentler dips farther westward. Three-fourths of a mile east of Kátsbaan, one of these abrupt changes in dip is finely exhibited in an old quarry in Becraft limestone at the road-forks.

On the road from Saugerties northwestward, a quarry has recently been opened for the production of road metal. It is in the Pentamerus and Tentaculite beds, which afford a superior material for this use. The limestones are much broken and fissured in this vicinity and the fissures are largely filled with veins of calcite.

40

The Onondaga limestone, west of Saugerties, extends along the road from Mt. Marion to Asbury in a belt averaging a quarter of a mile wide, lying on the eastern slope of the Beaver-kill valley. Exposures are almost continuous and some interesting features are presented. The most prominent outcrop is a line of low picturesque cliffs extending along the road for some distance south from Katsbaan. The limestone has been employed at several points for the manufacture of lime for local use. Near the road-forks west of Saugerties station there is a quarry in beds which are relatively free from chert. The rock is moderately hard, but owing to a tendency to vertical jointing and well-developed bedding planes it is easily dressed. Its color is a light blue-gray of very pleasant tint. The available beds of this quarry have a thickness of six or seven feet and these are accessible over a considerable area. A short distance southwest of Saugerties station, the railroad passes through a cut in the lower beds of the Onondaga limestone and runs on this formation from there to Kingston. The relation of the Esopus shales to the overlying limestones is well exhibited in this railroad cut. The black, slaty shales become lighter colored and calcareous, gradually lose their cleavage and give place to the argillaceous limestones of the base of the Onondaga. The limestones are exposed in the ridge east of the railroad to Mt. Marion station, south of which they are seen at frequent intervals in the railroad cuts. They dip gently to the westward into a wide valley filled with superficial formations, from which the Hamilton shales rise in high hills to the westward. In cuts adjoining the railroad bridge over Esopus creek, the impure basal limestones are again seen overlying the Esopus beds. The falls of the Esopus at this point are over a ledge of Onondaga limestone into a pool excavated in the beds of passage, and the Esopus shales are finely exhibited in the banks below. A short distance south of the falls a shallow synclinal is seen near the eastern edge of the limestones, but along the railroad the beds have their usual dip to the westward at angles of from three to fifteen degrees. Half a mile north of Katrine station the cherty beds of the limestone are exposed in a railroad cut. Their appearance at this point is shown in the following figure.

Fig. 8.— Chert layers in Onondaga limestone in cut of West Shore railroad, one mile north of Katrine station, New York.

West of the valley and flats underlaid by the Onondaga limestone there rise deep slopes of Hamilton shales which are remarkably continuous. These slopes rise 200 feet or more to terraces or a terrace-level of the harder flaggy beds of the overlying rim. Several creeks flow across this Hamilton shale region, of which the largest are the Sawkill and Plattekill, and these afford fine exposures of the formations. One particularly fine area is on the Plattekill a mile west of Mt. Marion station. Mt. Marion is of Hamilton rocks with a cap of flags.

The ridge of Helderberg limestones is deeply trenched by Esopus creek at Saugerties. To the southward it rises again, presenting a cliff of moderate height toward the plain eastward. On its westward slope there are outcrops of the upper Shaly and Oriskany formations, the latter sloping down to Esopus creek, to the west of which rise cliffs of Esopus shales. The relations of the Oriskany to the overlying formation along this creek are shown in plate 3.

In this illustration the Oriskany is seen in the low reefs to the right, with a reef of a harder bed of Esopus shales and steep banks of the slaty members on the left. The coincidence in the course of the creek with the strike of the rocks is a noteworthy feature, which is continued for over three miles. Near the road forks, a mile west of Glasco landing, the Helderberg beds are traversed by an anticlinal and synclinal entering the belt from the north-northeast. These give rise to small offsets in the line of cliffs, and the belts of outcrops at the gap through which the road passes to Mt. Marion station. These flexures widen and deepen southward; giving rise to considerable complexity in the distribution of the formations which they traverse. Their relations for the first three miles are shown in the following figure.

The distribution of the formations in this region is shown with considerable distinctness in the geologic map. The Becraft limestone is prominently exposed in this belt in cliffs twenty to thirty feet in height. It is of a light color, massively bedded, semi-crystalline in grain and very fossiliferous. The Oriskany is also exposed in great force and is remarkably fossiliferous. It is a silicious limestone with occasional streaks of chert, which is deeply weathered to a light snuff-colored, spongy rock, filled with casts and impressions of fossils. It is best exposed along the east bank of Esopus creek, below Glenerie, where the fossils occur in the greatest profusion along the road. As shown in the sections, the beds gradually pitch to the southward, and a mile north of Lake Katrine, the Oriskany sandstone pitches beneath the Esopus shales. This formation extends to the southward in a broad belt of rough ridges in which the flexures continue to the Kingston region. This belt has a high monoclinal ridge along its east sides constituted by Oriskany sandstone and the Helderberg limestones.

The Hudson river formation from West Camp westward is in greater part overlaid by clays and sands which constitute terraces extending from the high banks of the Hudson river to the ridge of Helderberg limestones. Along the banks of the Hudson and in the creeks which empty into it, there are many exposures, notably in the eastern part of the village of Saugerties. The formation consists of slates with interbedded, fine-grained massive sandstones, in layers from two inches to four feet in thickness. The slates vary from dark gray to black in color, and the

PLATE 3.

Esopus Slate on West Branch of Esopus Creek, above Saugerties, N. Y. Looking Down the Creek from the Bridge, One Mile East of Mt. Marion Station. Reefs of Oriskany Sandstone on the Right.

136

sandstones are of somewhat lighter tints. At the base of the Helderberg limestones the Hudson river rocks are exposed at only a few points. The localities near West Camp have been referred to, and there are a few others southwest of Glasco but their relations are not clearly exposed.

KINGSTON REGION.

In the Kingston and Rondout region the geology is particularly interesting and important. The cement beds are extensively mined and a series of flexures give considerable complexity to the relations of all the members. Prof. W. M. Davis[*] has given a brief description of a portion of the region, and a map showing some features of the distribution of the formations.

Mr. Lindsley[†] and T. N. Dale[‡] have described some of the relations at the cement quarries.

In the map and sections, plate 3, are given the data which were obtained in the region, and I believe they will fully illus- trate the general relations.

The principal features are the flexed, steeply-dipping monoclinal of the formations from the Salina to the Oriskany; the centroclinal area east of Wilbur which contains Esopus shales, and the corrugated folds of Esopus shales westward, con- taining a wide area of gently-folded Onondaga limestones, on which the greater part of the city is built. In this region there are many fine exposures of all the members, in numerous road, stream and railroad cuts, quarries and natural outcrops.

In the first section, on plate 4, are represented the relations which prevail northward to beyond Lake Katrine. A short distance south there are a series of excellent exposures into the eastern side of the ridge along an old tramway, and in an abandoned quarry to which it leads. The quarry is in the Becraft limestone which has been extensively excavated for lime burning. It is in thick beds dipping very gently westward. The lower limestone members are exhibited lying on the Hudson river slates in the railroad cut and some old cement openings near the turnpike. There is a four to six inch bed of impure ferruginous limestone

[*] The Nonconformity at Rondout; Am. Jour. Science, 3d series, vol. 26, pp. 389-395.
[†] Poughkeepsie Soc. Nat. Science, Proc., vol. 2, pp. 44-48.
[‡] Am. Jour. Science, 3d series, vol. 16, pp. 293-295.

containing Niagara corals. On this there lie seven feet of dark-gray limestones, impure near the base, and for two feet toward the top. Two feet above their bottom is a fossiliferous layer containing *Atrypa reticularis*, a very unusual occurrence in this part of the formation. This limestone is overlaid by a ten-foot bed of cement rock, of which the upper four feet are of poor quality. Next above is a heavy mass of fine-grained, dark-colored, brecciated limestone, filled with a great variety of corals representing the Stromatopora layer of the Tentaculite series. It has here the very remarkable thickness of ten feet with only a few thin beds of typical Tentaculite members above. These are overlaid by the heavily-bedded Pentamerus limestone, which, in the Kingston region, are quite cherty. A slight change in the strike in this vicinity is a notable feature, the relations of which are shown in plate 4. It appears to be connected with the anticlinal shown in section II of this plate. This anticlinal brings up the Tentaculite and cement horizons to the top of the ridge on the line of section II, and they are exposed just north of the road. The synclinal to the east widens to the southward, and holds an area of lower Shaly limestone which passes over the anticlinal and occupies a belt of considerable width in a series of rough ridges lying west of the crest of the main ridge.

Passing along the northern road over the ridge, there are extensive exposures of the upper and lower Shaly limestones with the intervening Becraft limestone, and the overlying Oriskany beds. The Shaly limestones present their usual characteristics of dark-gray, impure, moderately thick-bedded limestones, traversed by pronounced slaty cleavage. The Becraft limestone is in heavy beds, having an aggregate thickness of about thirty feet. The Oriskany consists of gray, very silicious, highly fossiliferous limestone above, with coarse sandstones below. The dips in this region gradually increase in steepness from the anticlinal, westward to eighty degrees in the Oriskany outcrops. The Oriskany beds give rise to a sharply defined subordinate ridge, extending along the slope of the upper Shaly ridge. To the westward there is a wide belt of Esopus shales which outcrop in a series of abrupt ridges of moderate height, but considerable steepness. There are several flexures on this belt, of which the character is shown in section on plate 4.

Returning to the eastern front of the ridge the cement bed is exposed in a series of old quarries, extending for some distance southward. In the slopes above this the Tentaculite bed with its Stromatopora layer is much less conspicuous than to the northward, surmounted by bare cliffs of the Pentamerus limestone.

The relations to the Hudson river shales are exposed at a number of points in the floor of the cement quarries and near the road forks northward. The shales dip steeply to the eastward and have a slightly irregular surface. This relation is not due to faulting but to deposition on a previously upturned and eroded surface, as shown by Davis in an exposure at Rondout.

On the road from East Kingston across the ridge there is a bank of clay and sand at the base, and then continuous exposure of all the members from the cement bed to the Esopus shales. The top of the cement bed is seen at the forks of the short road to the south, with Tentaculite and Pentamerus limestones in the slopes above. The lower Shaly limestone is in the crest of the ridge or constitutes a second crest just west, and is prominently exposed in the road cut. The Becraft limestone is well exposed in a small quarry on the east shore of a pond which lies in a depression in the upper Shaly members. This quarry exhibits twenty feet of light-colored, coarse-grained, massively bedded, very fossiliferous limestone, but the thickness of the member is somewhat greater, as shown in adjoining surface outcrops. On the west side of the pond the Oriskany formation rises as a small ridge of very sandy beds below and cherty limestones above, containing layers with Oriskany fossils. South of the road this Oriskany ridge coalesces with the main ridge and is separated from the Esopus shales by a hollow which extends for some distance southward. The Esopus shale region westward is a wide belt of high, rough, irregular ridges, which support a scanty vegetation and present an almost continuous outcrop of brownish-gray shales. On fresh fracture these shales are seen to be very dark gray or black, and the original bedding planes are obscured by slaty cleavage which is everywhere pronounced. The formation is traversed by the series of flexures shown in section II, on plate 4, and it is due to these that its area is so wide. The thickness is difficult to ascertain on account of the complexity of structure, but approximately it is not less than 275 feet.

On the east side of the Heiderberg ridge, south from East Kingston, there is a continuation of the line of high cliffs of Pentamerus and Tentaculite limestones, which rise from the terrace of clay and sand and trend nearly due north and south. The river has encroached upon the terrace in this vicinity, and a mile south of East Kingston extends to within a few yards of the limestone cliffs which continue near the river bank for some distance. In the brickyards in this region there are a number of exposures in which the clays are seen abutting against the limestones, and in plate 22 one of these is represented. The limestones shown in this plate are the Tentaculite and Pentamerus beds, and their dip is due west at an angle varying from sixty-three degrees to sixty-eight degrees. The overhanging cliffs were of course cut by the Hudson river before the deposition of the clays, and this exposure affords an interesting insight into a detail of the conditions that prevailed in this region in those times. The cement bed is completely buried under the clay from East Kingston southward, excepting at one point a short distance north of the quarry shown on plate 22 where a small stream flows out of the ridge and exposes rock nearly to tide water level. The cement was formerly worked near this outcrop, and the old adit by which it was reached extends under the road just north of the stream. The structure of the ridge in this region is shown in section II on plate 4, and the general relations shown in this section prevail for a considerable distance to the north and south. A short distance south the trend of the ridge changes to south-southwest and the river bank bears off to the eastward. The intervening terrace is an elevated sand plain underlaid by clay, and has a width of nearly a mile at Kingston Point. The lower members in the ridge are deeply buried under the clay and sand, but the upper limestones rise in a cliff or steep slope of considerable prominence. Approaching Rondout the terrace rapidly decreases in altitude and the eastern base of the ridge is again exposed. This is near the line along which section III of plate is drawn, and this section illustrates the relations of the western edge of the lower terrace on which Rondout is built.

It is in this portion of the ridge that the principal cement quarries of Rondout are situated. They extend continuously along the eastern slopes to the lower loop in the Ulster and Delaware railway, and penetrate far down the dip to the westward. The typical structure in this belt is shown in section IV, plate. 4. This gives place northward to an anticlinal, shown in section III. This begins as a sharp, somewhat faulted crumple in the monocline, which rapidly widens and pitches downward to the east and southeast. The cement rock was mined from the east-dipping limb, but as this portion of the mine had long been abandoned and there are no surface outcrops, I could not ascertain the precise relations northeastward. The anticlinal gives rise to a
• bench along the east side of the ridge, over which the upper road to Kingston passes diagonally. On the crest of this bench the Tentaculite beds are exposed, lying nearly flat, but they dip steeply down its eastern slope and pitch beneath the sand and clay of the terrace. North of the road the bench is terminated by a face in which a gentle arch of the Tentaculite limestone and cement beds are exposed. The cement is being mined from this face in a series of galleries extending to the westward. The west limb of the anticlinal is gently flexed by a low, local synclinal which is irregular in strike and not of great extent southward. The northern road to Kingston crosses the ridge in a partial gap in this vicinity, and the variations in strike are very noticeable in the Pentamerus beds along the road as well as in the cement beds in the mine below.

The formations constituting the ridge in the vicinity of sections III and IV, on plate 4, are the Helderberg limestones, the Oriskany sandstone, the Salina cement series, and the Hudson river sandstones. Mather,[*] Cook,[†] Lindsley,[‡] Dale[§] and Davis[‖] have described various features of this portion of the region and their statements are mainly accordant. The fact was recognized that the limestones lie unconformably on the Hudson river sandstones, and this feature is very clearly exposed at a number of

---

* Loc. cit.
† Geology of New Jersey, 1868, p. 156.
‡ A study of the rocks. Poughkeepsie Soc. Nat. Sci., Proc., vol. 2.
§ The fault at Rondout. Am. Jour. Sci., 8d ser., vol. 18, 1879, pp. 293-295.
‖ Nonconformity at Rondout. Am. Jour. Sci., 8d ser., vol. 26, 1893, pp. 389-395.

points. The Hudson river members are thickly-bedded, dark-gray, very fine-grained sandstones, with occasional thin shale partings between the beds. They dip south-southeast at angles from forty to sixty degrees and extend about half way up the slope of the ridge. Their upper surface is irregular, and Davis has given a figure illustrating an exposure in one of the quarries in which the limestones are seen fitting closely into channels worn along the strike of the sandstones, a relation which precludes the possibility of a fault. He adds: "It is noteworthy that the limestone begins immediately with its fully-determined calcareous character; there is no band of transitional composition; no fragments of the sandstone are contained in the overlying rock. The old, worn surface was swept clean before the corals and crinoids began growing upon it, and their fragments and grindings make the first deposit. Some little pieces of crinoid stems lie directly on the bare sandstones." The limestone lying above this unconformity is the dark-colored massive coralline bed which has long been known to be of Niagara age. Its thickness varies slightly, but averages seven feet. It gives place quite abruptly to the overlying cement series, but with no signs of a break in the sedimentation. The cement series consists of an upper and lower cement bed separated by a few beds of limestone. The thicknesses vary somewhat. The lower cement bed attains a thickness of twenty-two feet, which continues for some distance in the vicinity of section IV. The overlying limestones are here about three feet thick, and the upper cement bed five feet. Farther northward the lower cement bed thins and the intervening limestones and upper cement bed thicken considerably. The course of the cement series down the dip westward is shown by the broken lines C — C on the section in plate 4. Overlying the upper cement bed there are several thin beds of impure limestones containing *Leperditia alta* and, at their surface, prismatic mud cracks, as noted by Lindsley. The Tentaculite limestones have a thickness of about twenty-five feet, of which the upper six feet are classed as the ribbon limestone by Lindsley and contain *Stromatopora*. The Pentamerus limestone constitutes the crest of the ridge, and outcrops in cliffs of light-gray color. It presents its usual character of a lead-gray massive limestone, and carries a considerable amount of chert in courses and dissemi-

PLATE 5.

QUARRY IN BECRAFT LIMESTONE, KINGSTON, N. Y. LOOKING NORTH.

nated lenses. It contains *Pentamerus galeatus* and crinoidal fragments. Its thickness was not determined, but it is fully thirty feet as stated by Davis. The lower Shaly limestone extends along the center of the ridge with a thickness of about sixty feet, and the Becraft limestone lies high up on the western slope. Both dip steeply to the west. There are lime quarries in the Becraft beds which expose a thickness of about thirty-five feet of the usual heavily-bedded, light-colored, highly fossiliferous limestone, containg abundant calcite replacements of crinoid cups. One of these quarries, lying north of the road from Kingston to Kingston Point, is shown in plate 5. The upper Shaly limestones extend down the western slope of the ridge. The full thickness of the formation is well exposed near the end of the northern loop of the railroad, where the ridge widens somewhat, and here also there are excellent outcrops of Oriskany beds, which are more widely eroded southward. The upper Shaly beds have a thickness of about 125 feet. They are similar to the lower Shaly beds, and consist of brownish-gray impure limestones traversed by slaty cleavage. They are, as usual, sparingly fossiliferous, containing *Leptæna rhomboidalis*, *Stropheodonta radiata*, *Spirifer macropleura*, *Spirifer perlamellosus*, *Orthis oblata*, and others. The Oriskany formation is here extensively developed, and it contains a bed of conglomerate which, as stated by Davis, extends over a considerable area about Rondout. This bed consists of small pebbles, up to a quarter or a third of an inch in diameter, in a slightly calcareous sandy matrix. The pebbles vary from rounded to subangular and consist mainly of white quartz. It attains a thickness of nine feet at several points but is not continuous throughout. Its greatest development is just north of Wilbur in a steep hill slope near the bank of Rondout creek, but it is well characterized in the outcrop near the northern end of loop of the Ulster and Delaware railway. The upper beds of the formation are dark, hard, calcareous sandstones, with some cherty bands, which weather to a dull snuff-brown and exhibit abundant casts of many typical Oriskany fossils. The total thickness of the members in this locality is about thirty feet, which is a most unusual thickness for the formation. To the west of the Oriskany belt there are high ridges of Esopus shales — Oauda-galli grit.

South of the line of section IV (plate 4) the dips gradually decrease to fifty degrees. In about half a mile the ridge narrows and ends, and to the southward for some distance there are low lands and sand-covered slopes, in greater part occupied by the buildings of Rondout, an area in which there are no exposures. In the interval to Rondout creek there are several outcrops of Hudson river sandstone along the slopes just south of the main street, and a small showing of the upper and lower Shaly beds and intervening Becraft limestone, a short way beyond. These members and the underlying limestones and cement beds cross the Rondout creek half a mile northeast of the West Shore railway bridge and rise high in the bank on the south side of the creek. The Oriskany beds do not cross the creek but extend along the west bank on a long slope surmounted by Esopus shales. The conglomerate before described is a conspicuous feature of this exposure, and its area is extended somewhat by a small synclinal extending along the base of the slope. To the south the Oriskany beds pitch downward somewhat, and the overlying Esopus shales constitute the high bank for a short distance. They lie in a broad, gentle synclinal which pitches gently to the northward.

Approaching the railroad bridge a series of flexures come in which carry the Oriskany and Esopus beds westward and bring up the underlying limestones. They are finely exposed under the bridge and to Wilbur, in cliffs rising high on both sides of the creek. The relations at this point are shown in the following section taken from Davis's paper.

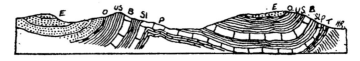

Fig. 4.—Cross section of Rondout Creek valley, just north of Wilbur, N. Y., after Davis. Looking north. E., Esopus shale; O., Oriskany sandstone; US., Upper Shaly limestone; B., Becraft limestone; Sl., Lower Shaly limestone; P., Pentamerus limestone; T., Tentaculite and cement beds; HR., Hudson formation.

The lower Shaly and Pentamerus beds are the most conspicuous features in these exposures, and they are finely exhibited. The Becraft beds are high in the adjoining slopes, where they have been extensively quarried for lime burning. In plate 6

PLATE 6.

HELDERBERG LIMESTONES ON NORTH BANK OF RONDOUT CREEK, AT WILBUR, N. Y. LOOKING NORTH.

a portion of the exposures along the Rondout
r.

es pitch gently downward to the north and pass
ed region occupied by a broad belt of Esopus shales,
ondaga limestones to the northwest. To the south-
ures are in the Hudson river shales under the low
of Wilbur, and the limestones extend southwestward
nal ridge of which the relations are shown on the
h V, plate 4.

Wilbur there is the basin-like area of which a cross
ven on the right of section V. I did not make an
ramination of this feature, for it appears to have been
explored by Prof. Davis. It is an extension of the
rhich crosses Rondout creek just north of the railway,
minates in about a mile in a "spooning up" of the dips.
includes the cement series, Helderberg limestones,
sandstone, and a small mass of Esopus shales. The
ore railway crosses its center and affords excellent
s of most of the beds. There are also a number of
exposing the Becraft limestone and cement series. The
bed is much thinner in this region than it is to the north-
and undoubtedly merges into the thin-bedded waterlimes
gested by Davis. The Niagara was not observed south of
ondout quarries. West from Wilbur along road and rail-
there is a section across the monoclinal belt, from lower
limestone to Onondaga limestone. The dips are steep
ough somewhat variable, but in the upper beds of the Esopus
es they flatten to ten degrees and the overlying Onondaga
estones lie in a very shallow synclinal. The Esopus and
ondaga beds are very finely exposed in the railroad cuts and
e intergrading of materials is clearly exhibited. The black,
aty Esopus shales gradually merge into impure limestones of
irty buff color, and these grade rapidly into the light blue-gray,
herty Onondaga limestones. The slaty cleavage extends for some
distance into the transition beds, but gradually gives place to the
massive bedding of the pure limestones. In the hollow just
west of these cuts the Esopus shales extend some distance north
where they pass under an arch of the limestone. From this region
to the west, north and the northeast there is an extended series of

shallow synclinals and low anticlinals in which the Onondaga limestones and Esopus shales are extended over a wide area. The general structure of this region is represented in sections II, III and IV, plate 4. The city of Kingston, excepting the Rondout portion, is in greater part built on the Onondaga limestone or on the sand by which this formation is deeply covered to the southwest. South of the Ulster and Delaware railroad there is a general pitch to the north, and the Esopus shales extend in long fingers northward along the anticlinals. These fingers unite around the ends of synclinals of the limestone southward, and the formation covers a wide area in the southwestern outskirts of the city and thence extends southward to the end of the great anticlinal of the Binnewater region. The Onondaga limestone area attains its greatest width near the line of section III, where it is not less than three miles wide from east to west. In this extension it occupies seven flexures, of which the westernmost are very broad and low, and pitch northward. They die out in the vicinity of Esopus creek, west of Kingston, for in the overlying Hamilton shales westward their only apparent influence is to change the direction of the general west-northwest monocline to north and north-northwest for a short distance. The pitch of the flexures in the northeastern section of the city is to the south, as shown in section II, and in these the limestone soon terminates in a series of fingers. Thence northward the principal flexures are in a broad belt of Esopus shales which is bordered westward by a west-dipping monocline of Onondaga limestone occupying a much narrower belt. This monocline is somewhat flexed locally and presents many minor, local variations in dip.

The most prominent flexure in the Kingston region is an anticlinal which begins near the West Shore railroad north of Wilbur and passes under the City Hall and along Clifton avenue by the almshouse. It is in Onondaga limestone from just south of Union avenue to near the almshouse, but is marked by long fingers of Esopus shales beyond, and at one point on the hilltop half a mile northeast of the City Hall this formation is exposed in a very small inlying area along the top of the arch.

Exposures of Onondaga limestone are frequent about Kingston, but they all lie to the southwest, south and east of the railway station, as the northwestern part of the city is heavily

PLATE 7.

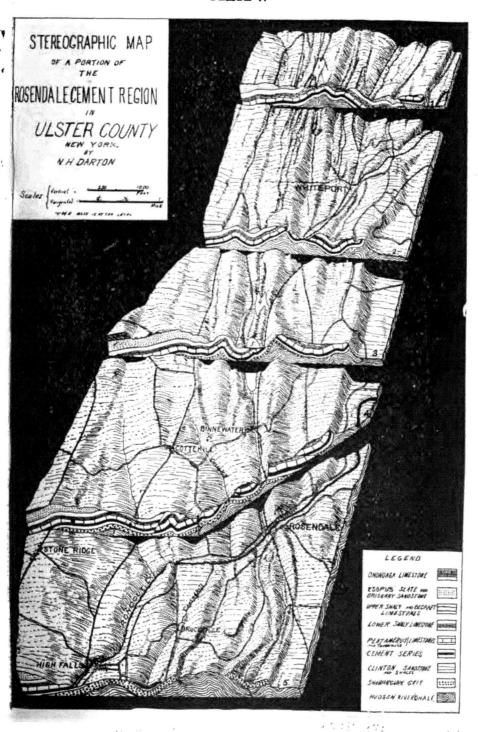

STEREOGRAPHIC MAP
OF A PORTION OF
THE
ROSENDALE CEMENT REGION
IN
ULSTER COUNTY
NEW YORK.
BY
N H DARTON

LEGEND

UofM

covered by a Champlain sand plain. Their location and the structural features which they present are shown by the dip marks on the map and by the sections. There are many exposures in the eastern part of the city, and in those near the Ulster and Delaware railway, east of the station, an irregular synclinal is seen, which extends across the principal axes of the north and south flexure. The dips are very variable along this belt and the beds are considerably broken. There are many veins of calcite in the fractured portions which give a rather unusual checkered aspect to the limestone.

Southwest of Kingston, up the Esopus valley, there extends a wide belt of Onondaga limestone. It is traversed by gentle flexures which extend from the southward and gradually die out north of Esopus creek. On the anticlinals the Esopus shales extend northward in fringes, and there are corresponding southward extensions of the limestone in the adjoining synclinals. The most prominent of these flexures are about Hurley. On the west side of the Esopus creek there rise steep slopes of Hamilton shales surmounted by terraces of the flagstone series. The slope is steep and continues for a long distance, but it is broken down for an interval west of Kingston. The beds are dark shales with intercalated thin sandy beds. There are many exposures north and west of Kingston in slopes and along creeks.

Southeast from Wilbur the monoclinal ridge continues for some distance along the north side of Rondout creek, presenting the general features shown on the left of section V, plate 4. The synclinal and anticlinal of Esopus shale west of this ridge pitch up to the southward, and, finally, the underlying formations are brought up in succession to the surface. These are, however, soon cut off to the westward by Esopus shales brought up by a fault which begins on the arch of the anticlinal and gradually crosses the ridge to the southward. The structure of this district was determined by Prof. W. M. Davis, and in the following figure a portion of his map is reproduced, which I believe fully illustrates the relations. I have introduced on this map a portion of the northeastern flank of the Rosendale-Whiteport anticlinal which was not shown on the original. The structure of the south end of the ridge is also shown in the first section on plate 7.

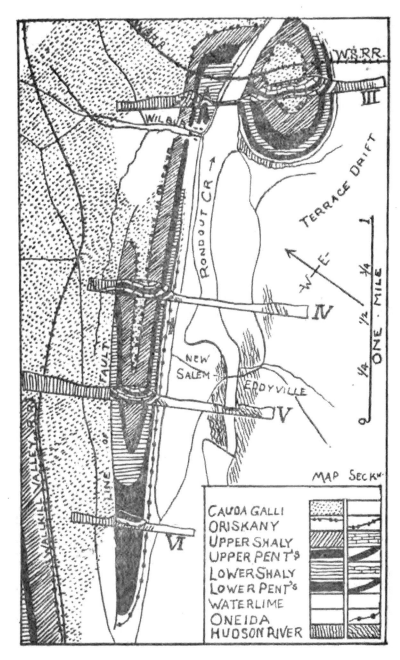

FIG. 5.—Map and sections of the southern part of the Kingston region, by W. M. Davis. Enlarged.

The eastern front of the ridge consists of cliffs of Pentamerus limestone, surmounting steep slopes in which the underlying formations are occasionally seen. The cement series is exposed at several points, but it consists almost wholly of the waterlime beds which contain occasional thin lenses of cement rock. The cement series is underlaid by quartzites which begin half a mile south of Wilbur and gradually thicken to eighteen feet in a couple of miles. Davis suggested that they are the Oneida or Shawangunk grit, but, as I have shown above, they are somewhat younger. Along the lower slopes there are occasional showings of Hudson river rocks, notably at a point behind New Salem, to which Davis refers and which is shown in his map. Here they are seen·overlaid by the quartzite and waterlime beds, and there is but little of the discordance in dips so conspicuous to the northward. There is some difference in the amounts, however, and this relation is, I take it, only a near coincidence of altitudes and not due to a less degree of unconformity.

The ridge ends a mile and a half south of Eddyville in a cliff of Pentamerus limestone facing to the south. Its termination is due to the fault which for some distance to the southward brings the Esopus shales against the Hudson river shales.

ROSENDALE–WHITEPORT CEMENT REGION.

The principal structural features of this region are shown in the stereogramic map and sections, plate 7, and the areal distribution of the formations is represented on the geologic map. There are two principal flexures comprising a great anticlinal extending through the center of the region, and a synclinal to the eastward; they carry subordinate flexures of varying degrees of magnitude and continuity. These flexures contain the cement beds, which come in again about Rosendale and Whiteport as rapidly as they thinned out about Rondout, and here attain their maximum development. As no determination has ever been made of the structure of this region, considerable time was devoted to its study, particularly of the cement beds, and many interesting structural and stratigraphic features were discovered.

The synclinal begins in the Kingston region and holds Esopus shales to just east of Whiteport station, beyond which the northerly pitch brings up the underlying formations in succession

along its axis.   The beds in the synclinal are cut off to the eastward
by the fault described above.   This fault gradually decreases in
throw southward, and passing out of the Esopus shales cuts off the
Oriskany sandstone and Helderberg limestones in succession along
the eastern limb of the synclinal, finally dying out at a point due
west of Creek Locks.   Near its termination the Clinton quartzite
appears to come in on the uplifted block, and the dislocation is
between this member and the cement series which pitches up
from below the Tentaculite beds west of the fault.   The fault is
covered by sand for a considerable distance in this vicinity, but
there is an exposure, apparently, of its termination, in an old
quarry in which the cement beds are seen slipped against a
slickensided, vertical face of the quartzite.   Near the surface the
bedding of both is conformable, but below, the cement series dips
steeply westward.

As the cement series comes to the surface it is seen to contain
thick cement beds, and these have been worked all along the
eastern side of the ridge to which the synclinal gives rise.   The
general structure of the synclinal in the vicinity of these workings
is shown in the second and third sections on plate 7.   The dips
are from fifty degrees to sixty degrees along the eastern crest of
the ridge, but they decrease westward and become flat for some
distance, then very gently anticlinal.   The road along the top of
the ridge passes along flat beds of Pentamerus limestones, which
are spread out over a considerable width by this structure.   In
the center of the ridge the dip increases, and the synclinal holds
a wide area of lower Shaly limestone which extends nearly to
Rosendale.   At their southern terminus they finely exhibit the
synclinal structure of the beds.   The principal cement bed has a
thickness averaging about twenty feet along the eastern slopes of
the ridge, and it has been mined very extensively.   It is massively
bedded and uniform in composition, with only occasional thin
cherty streaks.   It lies on the Clinton quartzite, and the relations
of this formation and the underlying red shales are very clearly
exposed in the adit to the New York Cement Company's quarry.
Here the quartzite is twenty-two feet thick, and it consists of
regular beds three to twelve inches in thickness, in greater part
welded together.   Their color is light-gray with buff-brown
streaks, and many of the beds have a characteristic minute cross-

bedding within themselves brought out by the slight differences in tint. The overlying cement is perfectly conformable and in greater part welded to the quartzite, but it is strongly contrasted by the great dissimilarity in materials, there being no transition beds and no intervening Niagara limestone. The shales underlying the quartzite are in greater part dull red in color, moderately fined grained, massively bedded as a whole, but breaking into shale on exposure and having a thickness of twenty-five feet. One or two beds are a dirty buff-tint in part, and at the top are two inches of gray shale which gives place abruptly to the quartzite. There appears to have been some slight slipping along this bed. About four inches from the top of the shale series here is a two-inch layer of breccia of small angular masses of cement-like materials in a gray-sand matrix. The lower part of the shales merge into two to three feet of dull gray-green grits, with blotches of pyrite and some small quartz pebbles, which lie on the Hudson river shales and undoubtedly represent the beginning of the Oneida or Shawangunk grit sediments. The dips at this opening are fifty degrees, and they decrease to forty-five degrees in the several quarries to the southward.

Rondout creek crosses the synclinal just below Rosendale, but does not appear to cut through to the cement near the axis of the flexure. At the point where the cement is crossed there are no outcrops, and for some distance to the southward the rocks are covered by sand. On the north bank of the creek there are cliffs of Pentamerus limestone in which the beds lie almost flat, and the formation extends up the slope southward on a gentle pitch to the north, which rapidly increases in amount to twenty degrees and twenty-five degrees. A short distance south of the river the synclinal "spoons out," the Pentamerus beds end in a line of low cliffs, and the cement beds outcrop at their base and circle around to the west and northwest. In section IV on plate 7, and in figure 11, there are shown the relations in the synclinal near its southern termination.

The cement has been quarried to some extent around the southern rim of the synclinal, and its relations are clearly exposed in these quarries, but elsewhere there is a heavy mantle of sand. The principal cement bed has a thickness of twenty feet and lies directly on Clinton quartzites. Near the entrance to the principal quarry the Shawangunk grit is exposed. Here it has attained a thickness of fifteen feet, is massively bedded, and its color has become white.

South from this region the western portion of this synclinal is continued in the Shawangunk grit, and in a local widening and deepening of the flexure, a mile and a half south of Rosendale, there is a small outlier of the cement bed obscurely exposed at several points. It crosses the railroad and extends around the end of a small local anticlinal which pitches up rapidly to the southward.

At Rosendale the western limb of the synclinal is traversed by a longitudinal fault which has offset the cement and associated beds to a considerable degree.

This fault crosses Rondout creek near the center of the village and extends up a depression to the northward, dying out in about a mile. Its presence is marked by a low cliff of Pentamerus beds along the canal and the juxtaposition of the upper part of the lower Shaly beds and the Pentamerus limestone a short distance north. To the south it passes into the Shawangunk grit area, where it was traced for some distance. Its maximum displacement is near Rosendale, where the amount is about 200 feet. Its general relations are shown in section IV, plate 7, and in figure 6. Some details of this overthrust are finely exposed in an abandoned quarry on the slope just south of the creek, opposite Rosendale, and it is on this exposure that the following sections are based.

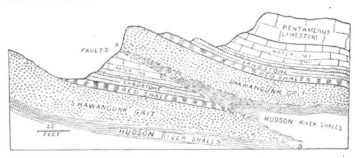

FIG. 6.— Cross section just south of Rosendale showing relations of overthrust fault. Looking north-northeast.

The wedge of cement has been worked out for a length of 200 feet, and the fault plane is the hanging wall of the quarry. Many minor details of the slate wedges and crumplings are not represented in the figure, but there is shown at D a small wedge of grit which is faulted into the main slate wedge at one point. The principal fault plane is along A–B, but there has also been considerable movement along A–C and in some of the beds above, which have slickensided the surface of the grit. The various small cross-faults and minor crumplings are irregularly intermingled in the displacement, and I did not attempt to work them out. The relations below the cement wedge are not fully exposed, but there are many scattered outcrops in the vicinity which exhibit the beds and their dips. This fault is probably the one referred to by Cook in his " Geology of New Jersey," * as a local inversion of the fold which has overturned the grit on to the cement. South from this point for some distance there are no outcrops exhibiting the relations of this fault, owing to the heavy sand cover. It crosses the railroad about a mile to the southward, and beyond this point its relations are clearly exposed in continuous outcrops of Shawangunk grit. It gives rise to a sharp cliff, which is conspicuous for about a mile and a half, and finally dies out, apparently with the termination of the fault. Its relations in this region are shown in the last section on plate 7 and sections I and II of plate 12. Owing to this fault the cement beds cross Rondout creek at Rosendale in two narrow belts. They are very near together and separated by small tongues of lower Tentaculite beds which are not clearly exposed. The easternmost cement belt pitches down to the northeast and is cut off by the Tentaculite and Pentamerus limestones along the west side of the fault. The western belt rises gradually to the northward along a northeast dip and extends continuously nearly to Whiteport on the east side of the valley, which is excavated along the arch of the Rosendale-Whiteport anticlinal. The eastern limb of this anticlinal is the western limb of the synclinal described in the preceding pages, and its relations are shown in the first, second, third and fourth sections on plate 7 and in figures 7 and 8.

The cement mines at Rosendale extend down the east slope of the beds and to the northward along the strike. The galleries

---

* 1868, pages 156-157.

begin at the western outcrop but there is also an outlet to the mines in an inclined adit which comes out in the depression just west of the fault. A portion of the western entrance to the galleries is shown in plate 8, and this plate also illustrates the relations of the two cement beds.

There are two cement beds in the Rosendale-Whiteport region, and at Rosendale the lower bed or "dark cement" averages about twenty-one feet in thickness, and the upper bed, or "light cement," eleven feet, with fourteen to fifteen feet of waterlime-stones intervening. The lower bed lies directly on the Clinton quartzite, the even upper surface of which affords an admirable floor for the galleries. For about eighteen inches at the bottom the dark cement is too sandy for use. With this exception and a few small layers of chert it is all available.

Overlying the cement beds there are several feet of waterlime beds containing thin cement layers. The Tentaculite and Pentamerus beds next above present their usual characters but are somewhat increased in thickness, and at Rosendale they give rise to a very high ridge presenting precipices to the south and west, as shown in and near the fourth section on plate 7. This ridge extends northward along the east side of the valley which occupies the crest of the anticlinal, and there is an almost con-tinuous succession of cement quarries along its western face. The formations dip gently eastward along this belt and have a very slight upward pitch to the north, which rapidly increases in amount near Binnewater station. The lower part of the valley is excavated through the Clinton quartzite and red shales to the surface of the Shawangunk grit, but farther northward it is in the Clinton quartzite. The cement beds also extend along the west side of the valley, and dip gently to the west-ward on the western limb of the anticlinal, where they are worked at several points. They are overlaid by Ten-taculite and Pentamerus limestones, which constitute the slope westward.

North of Binnewater station the axis of the anticlinal pitches up and the cement beds and overlying limestones are carried to a considerable altitude above the valley, as shown in section III

PLATE 8.

SOUTHWESTERN ENTRANCE TO CEMENT QUARRY AT ROSENDALE, N. Y.

362

on plate 7. The valley is cut laterally on the western slope of the flexure in this vicinity and exposes the Clinton members and the Shawangunk grit in a small inclosed area. The principal cement openings are high up on the slope, but the beds are also reached by an adit to which they descend on a steep easterly dip. This adit begins· in west dipping Shawangunk grits, crosses a small anticlinal of the underlying Hudson river shales, greatly contorted, and then penetrates the east dipping Shawangunk grit, and the Medina shales and Clinton quartzites to the cement. The cement rock on the western limb of the anticlinal outcrops along the center of the valley, and there are several openings along its course near the shore of the fifth Binnewater, west of the railroad. On the railroad in this vicinity there are extensive exposures of the Clinton and Medina members, notably in "Red rock cut," which is in the red shales. The first cuts expose the lower cement bed lying on twenty feet of Clinton quartzite. The dip is fifty degrees to the west-rorthwest. The quartzite is light colored, thin bedded and has the cross bedding by which it is characterized in the cement openings on the east side of the synclinal as described on a previous· page. The underlying shale series has a thickness of about twenty feet and consists of hard, massively-bedded, fine-grained, rather bright brown-red rocks, which break up into shale on weathering. The Shawangunk grit is a light-colored, quartzitic, massively-bedded quartz conglomerate, having a thickness of fifty feet in the adits to the cement mine, but it thins rapidly northward. In a short distance beyond "Red rock cut" the pitch of the anticlinal changes to northward, and the Shawangunk grit, red shales and quartzite are carried below the surface in succession. This is due to a small synclinal which crosses the principal flexure diagonally on a nearly due north and south trend. This small synclinal dies out a short distance south, but it widens and deepens northward and extends to beyond Hurley, where it is in the Onondaga limestone. The cement beds are extended over a superficial area of some width along this synclinal, and they have been widely removed from it along the railroad which crosses the ridge in a gap in this vicinity. In the following figure the relations of this synclinal are shown.

FIG. 7.— Cross section at the north end of the fifth Binnewater. Looking north. CG., Esopus shales; US., Upper Shaly and Becraft limestones; LS., Lower Shaly limestone; P., Pentamerus and Tentaculite limestones; C., Cement series; Cl., Clinton and Medina members; S., Shawangunk grit; HR., Hudson river shales.

Along the center of this basin, just north of the line of figure 7, there is a small tongue of Pentamerus limestone which extends from the northward across the railroad for a few yards at the south end of the fourth Binnewater. 'Along the shore of this Binnewater the Tentaculite and Pentamerus limestones arch over the cement on the anticlinal and dip west beneath the lower Shaly limestone.

To the north of this cross synclinal the eastern portion of the anticlinal pitches up again and brings to the surface of the valley, the Clinton and the Medina members, the attenuated Shawangunk grit, and a considerable area of Hudson river shales.

The cement beds have been worked all around the sides of this area and for a greater or less distance down the west dip. They are surrounded by the Tentaculite and Pentamerus lime-stones, except to the south along the axis of the anticlinal, where the valley is cut down to the cement series. In the following figure there is given a cross-section near the center of this district which illustrates the principal features. Further data in the portion somewhat north of this section are shown in the second section in plate 7.

FIG. 8 — Cross-section of the cement district one mile south of Whiteport station. Looking north. LS., Lower Shaly limestone; P , Pentamerus limestone; T., Tentaculite beds; UC., Upper Cement beds; LC , Lower Cement beds; C., Clinton quartzite; M., Medina shales; S., Shaw-angunk grit, and H., Hudson river shales.

The pitch of the fold is mainly in its western limb in this vicinity and the cement beds on the western side of the valley

PLATE 9.

CEMENT BEDS IN QUARRIES ONE MILE SOUTHWEST OF WHITEPORT STATION, N. Y. LOOKING NORTH.

are carried high up the slope of the ridge, where they finally attain a dip of sixty degrees to the westward as shown in the second section in plate 7. A short distance north of this section they pitch down again and are overarched by the Pentamerus and Tentaculite limestones along the eastern slope of the ridge. On the eastern limb of the main arch there develops in this district a gentle synclinal and anticlinal, which greatly widen the superficial area of the cement beds in the valley. They are shown to the right in figure 8. They do not extend far to the southward, but they extend north through the upper Binnewater district. They are well exhibited in the cement quarries and mines along the turnpike, south of Whiteport Station. The dips are not over five degrees at greatest on these flexures, and for the most part they are less than five degrees. North of the line of the second section (on plate 7) the cement beds in this shallow flexure gradually pitch beneath the Tentaculite and Pentamerus beds which occupy a wide region of low rocky ridges west of Whiteport.

In the cement region south of Whiteport there are the two cement beds, the upper or " white cement " having a thickness of twelve feet and the lower or " gray cement " eighteen feet, with seventeen to twenty feet of waterlime beds between them. The underlying formation is the Clinton quartzite, and this in turn is underlaid by the red shales, which in the northern part of the region are of a somewhat diminished thickness. The quartzite is in moderately thin beds of flesh-buff and pink colors of rather bright tints which are largely in ribbonings or mark a minute cross sub-bedding. The Shawangunk grit has a thickness of only three feet in the central part of the area and is a dirty brown to gray, pebbly quartzite. The best exposure of the formations underlying the cement series, and the only complete one, is along the railroad south of the southernmost turnpike crossing. A portion of this is shown in plate 9, which clearly illustrates the relations of the two cement beds.

In this plate the location of the Clinton shales is in the depression down the bank from the small boiler-house, the Shawangunk grit exposure is just to the right of this, near the railroad tracks, and the Hudson river shales are under the bridge. To the right of the eastern abutment of this bridge there is a wide valley occupied mainly by Hudson river shales and the Clinton members but in which there are no outcrops.

About Whiteport station and northward, the Rosendale-Whiteport anticline bears upon its flanks a series of flexures of various sizes, the relations of which are represented in the following figure.

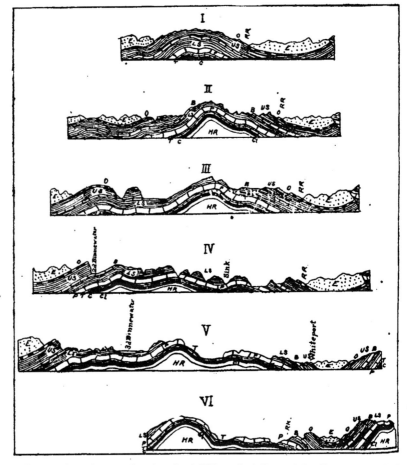

FIG. 9.—Cross-sections of region about Whiteport station and the Upper Binnewaters. Looking north. E., Esopus shales; O., Oriskany sandstone; US., Upper Shaly limestone; B., Becraft limestone; LS., Lower Shaly limestone; P., Pentamerus limestone; T., Tentaculite limestone; C., Cement series; Cl., Clinton formation; HR., Hudson river shales. Vertical scale considerably exaggerated.

It may be seen from the botton section in this figure that the cement beds are brought near to the surface over a considerable area in this region, and there are several small openings down to it. The pitch of the anticlinal is to the north and this finally carries the Helderberg limestone and Oriskany beds beneath the Esopus shales in the wide area of that formation south of Kingston. The region has been deeply eroded and it consists of a series of very sharp, rough, rocky ridges, due mainly to the wide extension of the upper and lower Shaly limestones. The upper Binnewaters, numbers 1, 2 and 3, lie in the valleys between the ridges northwest of Whiteport station, and there are several meadows, but the depressions are mainly deep, narrow, rocky gorges. The greater number of the ridges are not high, but their precipitous sides and the scrubby growth which they bear gives to the region a peculiarly wild aspect. · This roughness is by no means fully expressed in the stereograph (plate 7), which represents only the larger features. The principal ridge is along the highest arch of the anticlinal, but it is cut across diagonally by a valley near the center of the region, as shown in figure 9. The Binnewaters are beautiful little lakes nestled among the ridges in a most picturesque manner. They are more or less completely surrounded by cliffs or rocky slopes and have considerable irregularity in outline. The first or northernmost Binnewater is the largest and the second and third empty into it by separate outlets from the south. The second Binnewater is a very small body of water lying in a narrow gorge between the upper Shaly and Becraft limestones. At its head there is a meadow of some size and a small meandering stream which heads far northwest of the first Binnewater. This stream flows south between ridges of Esopus shales and the Oriskany sandstone and turning abruptly to the east passes through a small gorge in the Oriskany and upper Shaly limestone, beyond which it meanders northward through a meadow into the second Binnewater. The third Binnewater is in a valley which heads in a complex series of Shaly limestone hills to the southward, and it is some distance south of the second Binnewater. Its valley is separated from that of the second Binnewater by a long, narrow ridge of Becraft and lower Shaly limestones which ends in a point at the first Binnewater. The valley of the first Binnewater is in Esopus shales to the northward, and it extends along the western flank of the central axis of the anticlinal. In its course southward it cuts through a small arch of Oriskany beds in a short gorge, then flows through a region of upper Shaly limestone. At the head of the Binnewater there is a meadow underlaid by Becraft limestone and the lake basin is in the lower Shaly beds. The outlet is southward through a narrow gorge extending diagonally across the central anticlinal of the region, below which the brook turns eastward around a cliff of Pentamerus limestone and flows into a sink. Its waters come out again in a spring on the opposite side of a lower Shaly limestone ridge and flow past Whiteport station to the Rondout Creek.

The exposures in the upper Binnewater region are very numerous. The Oriskany beds are extensively developed as silicious and somewhat cherty limestones containing an abundant fauna. They extend along the Wallkill Valley railroad north from Whiteport station for several miles, and there are many excellent exposures of fossiliferous members in the slope on the west side of the track. The upper Shaly limestone constitutes many of the ridges south and west of the upper Binnewaters and a large portion of the slopes between the railroad and the road to Hurley, north of Whiteport station. It is a moderately dark-gray impure limestone, with the characteristic slaty cleavage which gives rise to very sharp ragged outcrops. It is moderately fossiliferous, and its thickness is about 100 feet. The Becraft limestone occupies several ridges south of the second Binnewater, the ridge between the second and third Binnewaters, the western and northern shores of the first Binnewater, and a portion of the cliffs and slopes of the high ridge northeast of the first Binnewater. It crosses the road to Hurley a mile northwest of Whiteport station, and extends along the second ridge west of the railroad to within a few yards of the station. It is the usual light-colored, thick-bedded, very fossiliferous limestone and has a thickness of thirty feet.

The lower Shaly limestone forms the central ridges of the upper Binnewater region and gives rise to the greater portion of the high ridge east of the first Binnewater. It is closely similar to the upper Shaly limestone but is not over sixty feet in thickness. The Pentamerus limestone occupies an area of considerable extent west of Whiteport, where it outcrops in low cliffs. It rises high in the ridge east of the third Binnewater and presents an escarpment to the eastward, as shown in the lower section in figure 9. In the valley at the foot of this escarpment the Tentaculite beds are brought up by an anticlinal over a small inclosed area and some pits have been sunk through their lower beds to the cement rock. This anticlinal extends into the eastern slope of the ridge southward, and this slope consists of an east-dipping mass of Pentamerus limestone to the line of the second section in plate 7, where the cement rock comes to the surface.

The Oriskany, upper Shaly, Becraft and lower Shaly beds cross the railroad just south of Whiteport station and extend to the southwest in the synclinal already described. The beds are all well exposed in the railroad cuts, the Oriskany outcropping just north of the station and the limestones a few rods south. Just behind the station there is a synclinal tongue of Esopus shales, which terminates less than a mile south, and in the slopes and ridge east there are upper Shaly, Becraft and lower Shaly beds dipping steeply westward as shown in the lower section, figure 9, and section II, plate 7. The Becraft beds are deeply quarried on the summit of the ridge and are well exposed at a number of points along the rim of the synclinal southward.

On the western limb of the main Rosendale-Whiteport anticlinal there are a number of flexures which come in from the north and northwest and gradually pitch up to the southward. They are first observed as low undulations in the Onondaga limestones and Esopus shales about Hurley, as before mentioned. They bring to the surface the Oriskany sandstones and Helderberg limestones in the region southwest of the upper Binnewaters, and along Rondout creek they bring up the cement series over a considerable area. Their general relations are shown in plate 7, and in part in figure 7. The first of these subordinate anticlinals westward is finely exhibited in a cliff at a point on the northern shore of the fourth Binnewater, where the upper Shaly and Oriskany members are flexed in a graceful arch. This flexure merges into the general anticlinal south of here and is lost. To the west of this flexure there is a synclinal holding a very narrow ridge of Esopus shales which extends to a point nearly west of Binnewater station. West of this synclinal there is an anticlinal of considerable prominence. It brings up the Oriskany in a symmetrically rounded ridge in a depression amid the Esopus ridges, in the fork of the roads a mile and a half due west of Whiteport. This ridge rises gradually southward, and in a half mile the Oriskany is eroded through on the summit and the upper Shaly and Becraft limestones constitute its crests to beyond the road from Binnewater station to Cottekill. Its structure is shown on the left end of the section in figure 7.

Rondout creek crosses these flexures above Rosendale, and the lower limestones and the cement beds are extensively exposed along its northern bank. The first synclinal west of Rosendale is the one that holds the long, narrow ridge of Esopus shales northwest of Binnewater station. It is a shallow basin in the cement rock, of which the bottom is near the level of the creek, and the beds have been worked to a considerable extent down both the slopes. On its western limb there is a small local fault which offsets the cement beds a few yards. Its relations are shown in the fourth section, on plate 7. In the anticlinal next west the Shawangunk grit rises forty feet above the creek bed and extends up the Cottekill. The cement beds and underlying formations are exposed on both flanks of the flexures and they cross the kill in succession a short distance above its mouth.

West of these flexures there are several others which rise in the region about Cottekill post-office and are of considerable prominence in the Rondout valley, as shown to the left of the middle of the fourth section on plate 7. They comprise two principal anticlinals, of which the easternmost crosses Rondout creek at the mouth of the Coxingkill and the westernmost at the big bend west of the turnpike bridge. The arch of the latter anticlinal is superbly exposed in cliffs of

PLATE 10.

FALLS OF RONDOUT CREEK OVER THE CEMENT BEDS, HIGH FALLS, N. Y. LOOKING NORTHWEST.

Pentamerus limestone along the creek and canal in this bend. Its character is illustrated in the following figure:

FIG. 10.—Arches of Pentamerus limestone on Rondout creek just west of the bridge on the turnpike from Rosendale to High Falls. A., south bank; B., north bank.

A short distance southwest there is either a slip or slight anticlinal in the general synclinal and not far beyond there is exposed in the canal bank, a low arch in lower Shaly limestone of which the western limb extends thence westward as a monocline.

The pitch to the northward is steep in the vicinity of Rondout creek in the Rosendale region and for some miles above and as shown in the following figure. The main arch of the Rosendale-Whiteport anticlinal brings up the Shawangunk grit south of the creek.

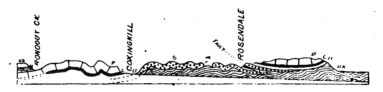

FIG. 11.—Cross section along the south side of Rondout creek through Rosendale. Looking north. US., Upper Shaly and Becraft limestones; P., Pentamerus and Tentaculite limestone; C., Cement series; Cl., Clinton and Medina; S., Shawangunk grit; HR., Hudson river shales.

From the highest arch, this formation is removed and the Hudson river shales extend nearly to Rosendale. Along the eastern side of the lower Coxingkill valley, the Shawangunk grits dip down a steep slope into a meadow underlaid by the Clinton and Medina formations and the cement series, as shown in figure 11. West of the kill there is a high ridge of Pentamerus limestone which extends to the Rondout creek where it exhibits the arch shown in figure 10. The eastern side of this ridge is a synclinal which widens considerably in the vicinity of Bruceville and continues up the Coxingkill valley far southward into the Shawangunk mountain. It holds the Clinton-Medina members, the cement beds and the Tentaculite and Pentamerus limestones for several miles, when the upward pitch finally brings the Shawangunk grit to the surface. The distribution of the formations in this flexure are shown on the geologic map and the structure is represented in the lower section of plate 7, and the two northern sections on plate 12. Two miles southeast of High Falls, the synclinal divides into two synclinals, with an intervening anticlinal ridge. The Coxingkill comes down the valley west of the ridge, and the outlet of Lake Mohonk is into a valley on the east side. Up the latter the Clinton and cement beds extend in a narrow belt, carrying in its center an outlier of Tentaculite and Pentamerus limestones which give rise to a small ridge. The cement series is covered by drift and debris in the greater part of the Coxingkill district and there is some doubt as to the boundaries, but it outcrops at the road forks south of Bruceville and it is mined near High Falls. These mines are in the western arm of the synclinal and the galleries extend for a considerable distance down the slope eastward. The cement is carried across the low ridge on which High Falls is built, by a wire rope tramway which extends to the canal. This ridge is due to Shawangunk grit, which rises a mile north of High Falls along a broad anticlinal in which are combined the flexures shown to the left on the fourth section in plate 7. The cement beds extend around the northern point of the ridge, cross the creek and canal a short distance above High Falls and continue northward along the west bank to the falls. They are not well exposed north of the village, but they cross the creek again to the west and give rise to the falls. These falls are shown in plate 10, and in plate 11 there is represented a portion of the north side of the gorge below, in which the members underlying the cement are finely exposed.

The principal cement bed in this vicinity has a thickness averaging fourteen feet. There is a thinner slaty cement bed below with a thin intervening series of waterlimes. The cement is

PLATE 11.

North Branch of Rondout Creek at High Falls, N. Y.; Exhibiting the Relations of the Clinton Formation. Looking Northwest.

worked in several quarries along the east bank of the creek above the falls. In the gorge below the falls there are forty feet of supposed Clinton to Medina members underlaid by the Shawangunk grit. The beds dip gently to the westward except at a small local anticlinal which crosses the creek near the falls, as shown in plate 11. The rocks in this exposure are principally. gray sandstones above and red shales below, with a calcareous sandstone bed intervening. The upper sandstones are thin-bedded and only moderately hard in texture. They contain several thin beds of shales of gray color and some of a dull red tint. The intermediate calcareous bed is about seven feet thick and gives rise to a small fall in the creek, which is shown in plate 11. It is a fine-grained, pyritiferous, cement-like rock, but rather more sandy than argillaceous. It is underlaid by a few feet of gray calcareous shales, which merge into the mass of bright red shales lying on the Shawangunk grit at the mouth of the gorge. These red shales contain intercalated beds of buff and green shales and have a thickness of about eighteen feet. They lie just east of the locality indicated on the right-hand corner of plate 11. Mather* described this section in some detail in his report on the first district, but he mistook the thin-bedded sandstones for lime-stones and I could not reconcile his statements with my observations. Cook, in the Geology of New Jersey,† gives some notes on this section which embody the principal facts.

The upper members in the High Falls gorge is quite unlike the quartzite which characterizes the horizon further northward and they represent considerably different conditions of deposition. Owing to lack of outcrops in the interval the gradation could not be studied.

The Esopus slates occupy a wide area west of Rosendale constituting a region of small but very rough ridges, in large part of bare rock. They are black, fine-grained rocks with pronounced slaty cleavage. On the road from Cottekill to Marbletown they are frequently seen and they constitute the ridge on which Stone Ridge village is situated. The structure is mainly a gentle monoclinal with low undulations, as shown on the left of the

---

* Loc. cit., pp. 353-354.   † Loc. cit., p. 157.

section of plate 7. These undulations are the beginnings of the flexures which extend southward into the Shawangunk mountain.

The Onondaga limestone occupies a long slope along a belt west of the Esopus shales. It is the usual light-blue gray cherty limestone. North of the Cottekill there are several outlying masses on the Esopus shales that are so large I have represented them on the geologic map. They average about twenty feet in diameter and appear to be in place. The dips of the limestones are very gentle to the west into the north and south valley of Esopus creek. West of this valley rise steep slopes of Hamilton shales, but these are deeply and widely trenched by the northwest and southeast portion of Esopus creek.

SHAWANGUNK MOUNTAIN.

The Shawangunk mountain lies between the Walkill valley and the southern Catskills. It rises gradually south from Rosendale and finally attains an elevation of 2200 feet and a width of five miles east of Ellenville. It continues to the southward with diminished width and height through New Jersey and Pennsylvania. In these States it is known as the Kittatining or Blue mountain, and it is crossed by the Delaware, Lehigh and Susquehanna water gaps.

The well-known summer resorts of Lake Mohonk and Lake Minnewaska are on the summit of the Shawangunk mountain in Ulster county so that the region has become familiar to a large number of visitors. Unfortunately, however, a description of its geology has never been published and the brief references in the report of Mather* throw but little light on the subject.

The structure of this mountain in Ulster county is a particularly interesting illustration of close relation of rock texture to topography, for the presence of the mountain and its form are directly dependent on the structure of a relatively thin sheet of hard rock. In the accompanying stereographic map, plate 12, an attempt has been made to represent its character, and its structure is shown in the cross-sections at the ends of blocks into

---

* Geology of New York; Report on the First District. 1843.

which the supposed model is divided. The mountain consists of a widely-extended sheet of Shawangunk grit lying on soft Hudson river shales. This sheet lies in a gently west dipping monocline which is corrugated by a series of gentle longitudinal folds. To the westward it dips beneath shales and limestones of the succeeding formations in the Rondout valley; to the eastward it is terminated by long lines of high precipices surmounting steep slopes of Hudson river shales. Its anticlinals give rise to high ridges and wide plateaus; its synclinals constitute in greater part the intervening depressions. In several portions of the mountain the grit has been eroded from the crests of the anticlines and the underlying slates are bared. This is the case in a wide area southwest of Ellenville, in a long strip extending from near Lake Mohonk nearly to Rosendale, in a small area east of Wawarsing and in the top of the mountain north of Lake Minnewaska.

The surface of the Shawangunk mountain is nearly everywhere very rugged, and it abounds in cliffs and rocky slopes. These consist of snow-white grits more or less mantled with dark lichens, and they are remarkably picturesque. There are numerous cataracts, many beautiful rock-bound lakes and widely extended views of the Catskills to the westward and the Hudson valley to the eastward. The ruggedness is due to the exceptional hardness of the rocks, the softness of the underlying shales and a tendency to vertical jointing, which gives rise to cliffs and clefts. There are low lines of cliffs all over the surface of the mountain, especially to the southward, but along the eastern face, where the grit is being continually undermined by erosion of the slate, they are of great prominence, in some cases having a height of 200 feet and extending continuously for many miles. The "points" are projections or promontories of the eastern edge of the grit beyond the general crest line, due to a less degree of recession. Buntico point, Paltz point, Gertrude's nose and Sam's point are the most prominent of these, but there are many others of minor importance. The lakes for which the mountain is famous lie in basins of considerable depth and are all near the top of the ridges. They are nearly surrounded by high cliffs of Shawangunk grit which present great variety of form.

The cliffs on the surface of the mountain are of various lengths and heights, and they are bounded for the most part by joint cracks. They face approximately east or west along the principal joints and north or south along cross joints, but there are some in other directions. They are usually in irregular steps on slopes and face each other and inclose depressions of various and varying widths on the plateaus. They are seldom continuous for over a few yards and merge into slopes or planes. The grits nearly everywhere present a basined surface. The basins are depressed an inch or two below the general level and are of various sizes and shapes. They usually contain pools of water and some sand and pebble detritus. They are mostly smooth and even polished, and all over the mountain, but particularly on its western slope, a large portion of the surface of the grit is smoothed or polished. These features are everywhere intimately associated with glacial scratchings and scorings and are probably due to glacial action.

The corrugations in the general monocline of the mountain are a series of anticlines and synclines which traverse the range diagonally from north-northeast to south-southwest and begin in succession from northeast to southwest, their axis rising gradually to the southward. Mather has suggested that the great cliffs of the regions are due to faults, but I find this is not the case. Only one fault was found and this was the small overthrust of the Rosendale region. There are many slight faults of a few inches or feet, but they appear to be entirely in the grit. Begininng at the northern end of the range the principal feature is the anticlinal which brings up the cement beds between Rosendale and Whiteport, as described in a preceding chapter. South of Rondout creek, opposite Rosendale, the upward pitch of this flexure increases rapidly and the Shawangunk grit soon rises into a ridge of considerable altitude. In a short distance from the creek the grits are eroded from the crown of the arch, and to the southward the underlying shales constitute a series of high hills extending along the center of the mountain. The occurrence of these high hills of soft rock is a

PLATE 13.

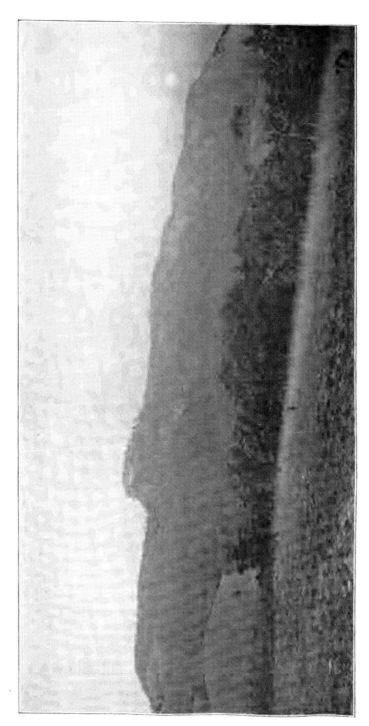

BUNTICO POINT, LOOKING NORTH.

striking feature. Their existence is due to the former protection of the arch of Shawangunk grit by which they were originally covered. The grit in the flanks of this arch extends down the slopes of the mountain where it dips beneath the overlying formations in the valley on the west side, and extends nearly or quite to the base on the east side. One mile and a half south of Rosendale the mountain has the structure shown in the first section on plate 12, in which it will be seen that the sheet of grit lying along the eastern slope of the mountain is considerably corrugated. This corrugation consists in the main of a western limb dipping more or less steeply eastward and a shallow synclinal, which, at one point, holds a small area of the cement series. At the southern end of this cement area there is a very abrupt anticlinal crumple in the synclinal which extends but a short distance in either direction and then flattens out into the general flexure. The fault extends from the Rosendale cement region and gives rise to a sharp ridge which continues to the first road across the mountain, beyond which it dies out. Along the eastern face of the eastern range of the mountain the dips are in greater part gently to the westward. Along the railroad they are twenty degrees and this is the average for some distance; on the first road across the mountain the dips are sixty degrees, but this steep dip soon gives place to inclinations of not over ten, and toward the southern end of the ridge the synclinal dies out and there is a general, very gentle dip to the east. This grit area lying along the eastern slope of the mountain terminates very abruptly southward in a line of cliffs, and owing to a general pitch which has carried the beds upward to the south, these have great elevation. The cliffs are known as Buntico point and it is one of the most prominent topographic features in the region. Its principal relations are shown in plate 13.

In this plate there is shown the end of the narrow Shawangunk grit area, and a portion of its eastern face which extends diagonally down and along the slope of the mountain to the right. It is terminated on all sides by cliffs, under which the Hudson river shales appear, and these shales constitute the high hills of the center of the mountain to the left, over which the grit originally arched. Unfortunately the photograph from which plate 13 was reproduced was taken under unfavorable conditions and is not as clear as could be desired.

South from Buntico point the eastern crest of the Shawangunk mountain consists of a great mass of soft Hudson river shales which are being rapidly and deeply eroded. They extend south nearly to Lake Mohonk, where the crest of the anticlinal is occupied by grit for some distance.

The grit in the western limb of the anticlinal lies along the western slope of the northern end of the mountain and does not attain the prominence that it has in the ridge terminating in Buntico point. It constitutes a monoclinal ridge with a line of cliffs along its eastern edge above which the hills of Hudson river slates rise several hundred feet. About the northern end of the mountain the grit of this monoclinal extends eastward over a series of shallow flexures which pitch rapidly to the northward, as shown in figure 11. The hills of Hudson river shales sink rapidly in this portion of the region and soon give place to a rocky, undulating plateau of Shawangunk grit which closes over the end of the anticlinal in the vicinity of Rondout creek. To the west of the west-dipping monocline of Shawangunk grit there is the synclinal valley of the Coxingkill, containing overlying members up to the Pentamerus limestone, which was described on a previous page. On the opposite side of this valley, at High Falls, there rises one of the principal anticlinals of the Shawangunk mountain, which soon brings up Shawangunk grit in the low ridge on which the village is built. This ridge gradually increases in width and altitude southward, and near the line of the third section on plate 12 its crest is nearly as high as the ridge eastward, from which it is separated by the synclinal valley of the Coxingkill.

South from Alligerville the mountain widens rapidly as flexure after flexure brings up the Shawangunk grit from the northwestward. The western ridges rise gradually with the upward pitch of the axes of the flexure and finally become the highest part of the mountain east of Ellenville. Southwest of Lake Mohonk the range comprises five of these flexures, together with various small undulations of the beds, and there is a creek in

PLATE 14.

CLIFFS OF SHAWANGUNK GRIT ON THE WEST SIDE OF LAKE MOHONK.

each synclinal. Lake Minnqwaska is in the crown of the anticlinal, which rises at High Falls, and Lake Awosting is on the
western slope of the same flexure.

These lakes are all situated near the eastern side of
the mountain and about 150 feet below the crest. They are
similar in relations and originated under almost the same
conditions. Lake Mohonk occupies a north and south cleft
in the crown of the anticlinal which rises at Rosendale.

The structure of the lake is shown in the following
figure :

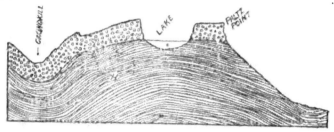

FIG. 12.— Cross-section of eastern ridges of Shawangunk mountain through Lake Mohonk.
H., Hudson river shale. Looking north. Vertical scale exaggerated.

The lake basin is in Hudson river shales but it is surrounded on
the east and west by high cliffs of Shawangunk grits. To the
south there is a gap in the front of the mountain through which
the shales extend to the lake. The top of these shales is a few
feet above the surface of the lake at its southeast end but the
pitch carries them a few feet below the water surface to the
north and west.

The view in plate 16 is looking southward and through the gap
in the east front of the mountain through which the Hudson
river shales extend to the lake. On the left is Paltz point and
to the right in the distance there is "Cope point" a projection
of the southern extension of the eastern front of the mountain.

East of the lake there is a thick mass of grit which lies along
the crest of the anticlinal. It begins a short distance north and
is terminated by very abrupt cliffs in Paltz point near the
southern end of the lake. The character of this "point" is shown
in plate 16, and its relations are represented in the stereogramic
map.

At the head of the lake and the base of the south end of the
mass of grit at Platz point the Hudson river shales constitute a
small plateau which surmounts the long eastern slope of the
mountain. There is no cross drainage way at the base of the
cliff, and the cause of the abrupt termination of this point is difficult to understand.

The grit dips gently to the west northwest along the west side
of Paltz point and very slightly to the eastward in the easternmost part of the range. Northeast of the lake the dip is at a low
angle to. the westward, but there are several slight undulations.
There is everywhere a pronounced pitch to the northwest. Owing
to the westerly dip the grits in the Paltz point ridge are somewhat lower just north of the.lake than elsewhere. It will be
seen from these statements that the lake lies slightly west of the
center of the arch of the anticlinal and all the dips along its
shores are to the northwest although at very low angles. The
degree of dip rapidly increases down the western slope of the
mountain to the synclinal valley of the Coxingkill.

The outlet of Lake Mohonk is to the northward by a branch of
the Coxingkill. This branch flows through a slight depression
separating the Paltz point range from the main mountain mass,
and then obliquely down the flank of the anticlinal.

South from Paltz point the eastern front of the mountain presents a nearly unbroken line of cliffs for many miles along or
near the crest of the anticline. The nature of a portion of the
escarpment is shown in plate 17.

Two miles south of Lake Mohonk there is a slight depression
in the crest line through which the road to Lake Minnewaska
passes and there are several other depressions of less amount.
Millbrook mountain is the culminating feature of the portion of
the range beyond which its front is somewhat more irregular in
contour.

Lake Minnewaska is similar to Lake Mohonk in appearance,
but it is somewhat larger. It was not ascertained whether its
basin extends into the Hudson river shales, for there is a continuous rim of grit surrounding it. As a very great thickness of
grit is exposed above the water level in this vicinity it seems
probable that the bottom of the lake is very near the shales.
This probability is increased somewhat by the presence of the

PLATE 15.

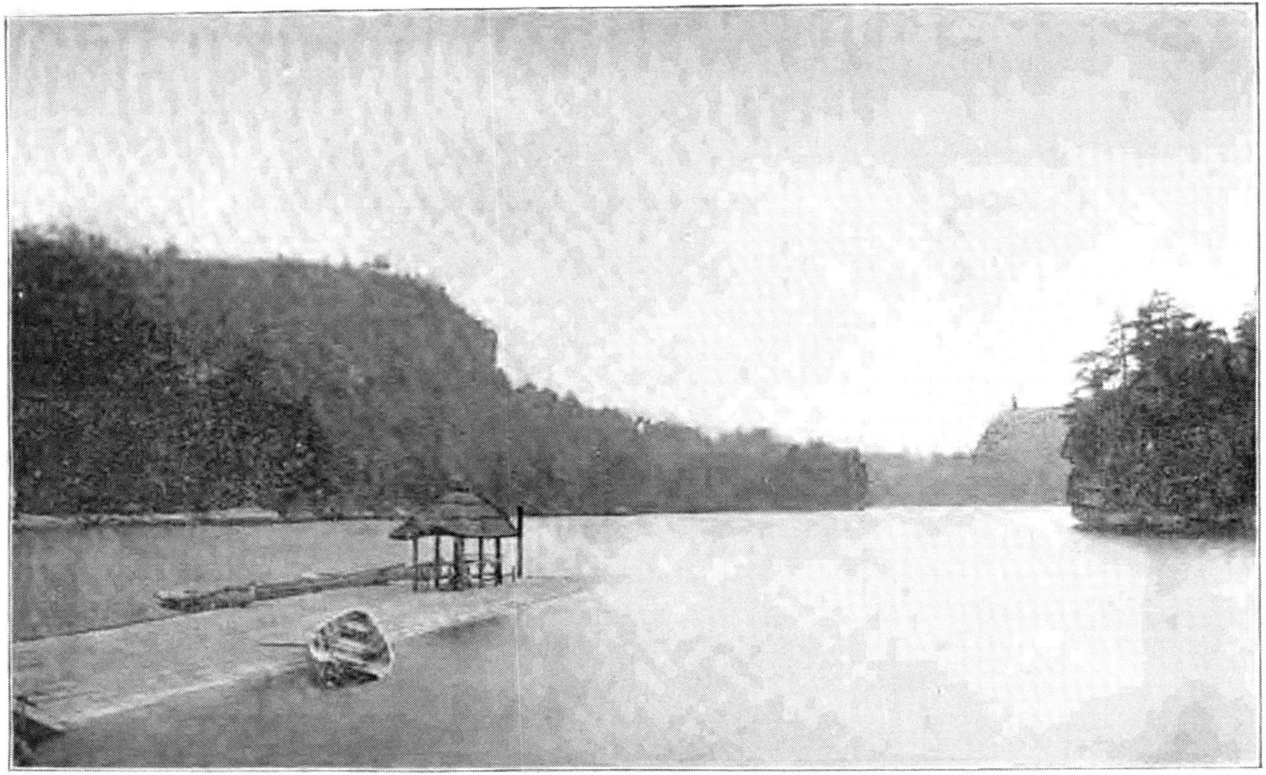

LOOKING UP LAKE MOHONK. PALTZ POINT ON THE LEFT.

Ῑ

steep cliffs and the width of the valley or cleft in which the lake lies. In the following figure there are shown the principal structural features at this locality.

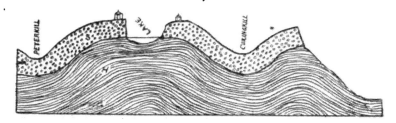

Fig. 18.— Cross-section of the eastern ridges of Shawangunk mountain through Lake Minnewaska. Looking north. H., Hudson river shales. S., Shawangunk grit.

The cliffs which extend along the east side of the lake are very high and precipitous. They are shown in greater part in plate 18. As at Lake Mohonk the rocks are greatly fissured and they are traversed by many deep, wide clefts. The dips are gently anticlinal about the lake, which is on the axis of the flexure, but they increase in amount to the east and west.

The lake empties to the southward through a wide gap into the synclinal valley of the Coxingkill, and it may be regarded as the headwaters of this stream.

A mile southeast of the lake the anticlinal in which the lake is situated is crossed by the road to Port Hixon, and in the vicinity of the road the grit has been eroded from the crown of the arch for some distance. The road crosses the ridge in a gap on the Hudson river shales, and the edges of the grit give rise to high cliffs on either side. Down the slope the grit outcrops on the flank of the arch, but the slate extends along the slopes of the mountain for some distance, especially on the east side. The occurrence of the slate in this inlying area is a very striking feature, and the reason for the removal of the grit at this locality is not clear.

South of Lake Minnewaska the front of the ridge trends to the southwest for some distance, and the Coxingkill synclinal and the Minnewaska anticline pass out to the south. There is a prominent "point" in this vicinity known as Gertrude's nose, which is due to a deep incision in the front of the mountain made by a small branch of the Wallkill. This stream heads in the plateau south of the lake, passes over the edge of the grit in a series of falls, and has cut a deep gorge into the Hudson river shales below.

Lake Awosting is the largest lake of the series and is a considerable body of water. It is mostly surrounded by low cliffs and rocky slopes, but near its eastern end there is a very high cliff for some distance which comes in from the crest of the mountain eastward and constitutes a high west-sloping plateau northeast of the lake.

In the following figure there is given a view of this lake, based on a kodak photograph.

FIG. 14.— Lake Awosting from the east-northeast.

The basin of this lake does not appear to be in Hudson river shales, though possibly they underlie its deeper portions. The grit dips gently west along the shores, and this dip continues over a wide area. To the west is a long slope which extends from a low cliff along the lake to the main Peterkill or Vly Creek valley.

The outlet of the lake is by a branch of the Peterkill which flows along the west sloping grits for a mile and then passes over high falls into the main valley of the Peterkill. To the east of the confluence there is a narrow depression known as the "dark hole," which extends southeastward up the slope of the mountain. It is bordered by moderately high cliffs of east-dipping grits and was cut by a stream which empties into the Peterkill. On its south side is the high plateau of which the eastern front is the cliff at the southeast end of Lake Awosting. Its relations are shown in the stereogramic map.

The Peterkill valley, from beginning to end, flows on the western flank of the anticlinal on which Lake Minnewaska is situated. It has a cliff of west-dipping grit along its west side

PLATE 16.

SOUTH END OF PALTZ POINT. LAKE MOHONK IS IN THE DEPRESSION TO THE LEFT.

and long slopes of grit to the east. Four miles below Lake Awosting the kill passes over "Awosting falls" and then over a series of cascades aggregating in all a fall of 240 feet (approximated). In the Awosting falls there is a clear drop of sixty or more feet. In plate 19 these falls are shown. They are a mile north of Lake Minnewaska and are an attractive feature of that resort.

In the bottom of the gorge below the several falls there are high cliffs of grit for some distance. Owing to a considerable pitch to the north, or down stream, and a thickness of grit somewhat over 200 feet, the falls of this series do not cut through to the Hudson river slates.

South of Lake Awosting there are two small ponds on the summit of the mountain, but I did not visit them. Mud pond is one, at the head of Vly Creek or the principal branch of the Peterkill, and Lake Maratanza is the other. Lake Maratanza empties to the east by a branch of the Wallkill, which pitches over the edge of the mountain a short distance from the lake in a great fall, and into a deep gulf of Hudson river shales. The locality is known as Verkeeder falls and it is said to be a very fine feature.

Between Gertrude's nose and Sam's point the crest of the mountain is very high, but for some distance the edge of the grit is broken into great terraces, and there is a sloping bench of Hudson river shales of some width at their base. Several branches of Walkill drainage head in the crest of the mountain in this region and pass over the edge of the grit in falls, of which the above-mentioned Verkeeder falls are the most noteworthy.

In this region the mountain continues to narrow and most of the flexures pass out to the southward. This narrowing is due to the recession of the edge of the sheet of the Shawangunk grit and is closely related to the upward pitch of the flexures. This pitch increases the height of the mountain southward, but with increased height there is a corresponding increase of erosion in the soft underlying shales, which beyond certain limits causes rapid recession. This is illustrated by Sam's point, where the maximum altitude of 2200 feet is attained. The "point" is a narrowing extension of the grit along the axis of a very flat synclinal, which finally terminates in a high narrow cliff pre-

sented southward. From the wide anticlinal area to the west
the grit has been eroded and the Hudson river shales occupy the
surface in a group of very high hills. These hills are surrounded
on the east, south and west by cliffs of the grit which rise somewhat above them to the east are about even with their higher
summits on the north, and lie on their flanks to the west. It is
the grit on the western limb of the anticlinal that lies on the
western flanks of the slate hills, and this relation continues in a
monoclinal mountain which extends from Ellenville far southward into Pennsylvania. This monoclinal mountain consists of
a single-crested ridge of the Shawangunk grit with a long slope
up the dip from the valley to the west, which terminates in an
east-facing cliff of grit surmounting long rolling slopes of shales
on the east side of the mountain. Its structure near the southern edge of Ulster county is shown in the bottom section on
plate 12, and this is typical for the greater part of its course.
The dips along the western slope of the mountain are low north
of Wawarsing, but they rapidly increase southward to an
average of about sixty degrees in the vicinity of Ellenville. In
this region of steep dips the streams flowing down the steep
western slope have cut deep gorges, which in several cases
extend through the grit into the underlying shales. The two
streams south of Ellenville are exaggerated examples of this,
and they have been largely instrumental in baring the Hudson
river shales on the anticlinal axis behind Sam's point. The two
streams just north of Ellenville also cut down to the shales, but
they are small and have cut only narrow gorges. Opposite
Napanoch there is a small creek which cuts a deep gorge into
the shales, and in the higher part of the slope has bared an area
of considerable size, which is surrounded by great cliffs of the
grit. The stream opposite Wawarsing has cut a gorge and
removed a portion of the grit in its upper portion, but does
not cut through to the slate. The head of this depression
extends into the head of the depression opposite Napanoch,
and they are surmounted on the east by a continuous line
of high cliffs. The stream which flows out of the mountain
at Port Hixon is larger than the others and has cut a deep
wide gorge, but owing to the lower dip of the grit it does not
appear to have cut through to the shales to any great extent.

PLATE 17.

Eastern Face of Shawangunk Mountain from near Lake Mohonk to Millbrook Mountain. Looking South-southeast.

100

No shales were observed in places in the depression, but a small amount of shale debris was noticed at one point. Everywhere along the steep slopes there are clefts in the grit, some of which appear to extend down to the shales. One of these is the "Ice Cave," a locality which is widely famous in the region. It is high in the slope about two miles east-northeast of Ellenville. Ice and snow remain in it in greater or less amount and in some seasons are preserved entirely through the summer and autumn. The top of the mountain southwest of Wawarsing is a wide plateau which is traversed by the valley of Stony creek. Its surface is very irregular and consists of low cliffs of the base grit.

The relation of the Shawangunk grit to the Hudson river shales in the Shawangunk mountain region is one of slight but persistent unconformity. The coarse grit lies directly on the slate and there is an intervening eroded surface. This erosion has truncated low arches of slate but channeled its surface only slightly. Exposures of the relations are everywhere abundant. One of the best instances is along the road from Minnewaska to New Paltz, at a point two miles south of Lake Mohonk. Here along the mountain slope a very low arch of the grit is exposed with underlying shales in an arch that is plainly seen to be materially steeper. There is divergence of dip in nearly every locality, varying from very slight to ten degrees, but several points were seen where it was hardly perceptible.

The origin and history of the lakes is not entirely clear, but they appear to be due to glacial agencies. The principal feature has been a local deepening and widening of a pre-existing valley, aided, in the case of Lake Mohonk at least, by the presence of shales at the point now occupied by the lake. They do not appear to be due in great measure to damming by glacial or other debris, or to dislocation.

Owing to its prominence the mountain has been long exposed to erosion. Originally the grit was overlaid by a great mass of limestones and shales and the rocks of the Catskill mountain, but these were removed far down into the Rondout valley at an early period. During the glacial epoch there was extensive erosion and the removal of great masses of the grit, some of which are now found in the glacial drift far to the southward. The surface of the rocks was scratched, scored and polished by the pebbles and sand in the bottom of the glacier and these features are conspicuous all over the mountain. Some further account of them will be found on a subsequent page. To the glaciation, too, is probably due the abruptness of Paltz point, the steplike structure over the surface of the mountain and other features of that sort. The sheet of grit originally extended far to the eastward, but by long-continued undermining of the soft underlying shales its front has gradually receded to its present position. This recession is still actively in progress, and every year there fall great masses from the front of the mountain. One of the regions of weakness is Paltz point, for the shales at its base are exposed to erosion on several sides and fragments of the grit will fall off as the undermining progresses until finally the mass will disappear. Probably before it is gone the streams heading near its southern end will cut back through the slates at the head of Lake Mohonk and this beautiful body of water will be drained off. Of course this is all very remote as human history goes, and artificial means will stay its progress in some measure; but it will all be accomplished in the near future, geologically speaking. Lakes Minnewaska and Awosting lie so far back from the front of the mountain that they will survive Lake Mohonk a long time.

THE RONDOUT VALLEY FROM ABOVE HIGH FALLS TO ELLENVILLE.

The most prominent features in this valley are wide areas of superficial formations which cover the underlying rocks. These rocks comprise the several members from Onondaga limestone to Clinton shales, but owing to the drift covering they are but rarely exposed. Their distribution as shown on the geologic map is in great part based on widely separated exposures and there are areas of considerable size for which there is no definite information as to the distribution of all the beds. The structure of the region is a monocline dipping to the northwest and west. The strikes are northeast to the vicinity of Port Jackson, east-northeast to Port Hixon, and north-northeast to Ellenville and beyond. The dips are very gentle north of Port Jackson, but they gradually increase in amount to the southward. At Wawarsing, the maximum dips average thirty-five degrees; at Napanoch forty-five degrees; at Ellenville forty-five degrees; and they continue at this altitude beyond Homowack. The

PLATE 18.

LOOKING DOWN LAKE MINNEWASKA, N. Y.

steepness of this dip gradually decreases westward and gives place to a very gentle inclination to the westward. It also decreases to the eastward on the summit of Shawangunk mountain. The southern and eastern side of this valley is the long western slope of the Shawangunk mountain with its bare flanks of Shawangunk grit. To the westward are long spurs of the foothills of the Catskills. •

A mile west of High Falls, just west of the turnpike to Ellenville, there are exhibited in hill slopes the lower Shaly, Becraft and upper Shaly limestones and a short distance south the lower Shaly beds are seen along the turnpike. Along the ridge westward on the road to Kripple Bush, the Becraft and upper Shaly limestones are seen, capped by the Oriskany which extends over an area of considerable width sloping to the westward. This area is succeeded by a sharp rise due to a wide ridge of Esopus shales, which is a marked feature from Stone Ridge for twelve miles southward. The Esopus formation here consists of very hard dark slates which merge into an upper member of dark slaty sandstones. On the western slope of this ridge, as in the region northward, the Onondaga limestones extend to a valley of considerable width, in greater part heavily covered with drift. The relations of these features in the exposures extending from Kripple Bush eastward are shown in the following figure:

FIG. 16.— Cross-section from the Rondout valley to a point beyond Kripple Bush. Looking north. S., Shawangunk grit; Cl., Clinton and Medina shales; C., Cement series; T., Tentaculite limestone; P., Pentamerus beds; L., Lower Shaly limestone; B., Becraft limestone; U., Upper Shaly limestone; O., Oriskany limestone; E., Esopus shales; On., Onondaga limestone; H., Hamilton shales.

The Clinton and Medina shales are rarely exposed in this valley, and the description of their occurrence at High Falls will answer for the entire region so far as I have seen them. The cement bed was not found between High Falls and Port Jackson, as the creek apparently runs over drift lying in a trough excavated along the cement horizon. The Pentamerus beds

were not seen between High Falls and Accord, but it is probable
that they underlie a well-marked terrace which extends near the
turnpike. Between Accord and Pine Bush they are exposed
at several points in low cliffs by the turnpike. At Port Jackson
there is a low anticline extending from the western ridge
of the Shawangunk mountains, and the Pentamerus beds rise
on its western flank, giving rise to a short ridge of moderate
prominence with cliffs of limestone fifty to sixty feet high. The
Tentaculite limestone and cement beds are obscurely exposed at
the base of the southeastern side of this ridge. The cement is
said to be of considerable thickness and excellent quality, but the
outcrops were too obscure for me to ascertain the correctness of
these statements. Stony creek passes just south of this ridge,
and on the opposite side of the creek there are exposed the red
beds of the Clinton formation, outcropping over the point of the
anticlinal, which is here pitching quite steeply to the northeastward.

The lower Shaly limestone was not observed in this region or
southward. The Becraft limestone was seen, however, at a
number of points presenting its usual characteristics of a light-
colored, semi-crystalline, massively-bedded limestone, containing
an abundance of fossil shells. Its thickness appears to be considerably diminished, although no complete sections were found.
On a hill just south of Millhook, the outcrops cover a considerable
area and at this point and in the vicinity it has been burned for
lime. The Oriskany sandstone is exposed at Millhook at the
milldam. It consists of a very dark silicious limestone below
with dark quartzites above. At the locality above referred to,
southeast of Kripple Bush, its thickness is at least ten feet and at
Millhook it is about the same. The Onondaga limestone has been
extensively quarried at many points in this valley, between Stone
ridge and Kripple Bush, at Whitfield, about Pattankunk, at
Wawarsing and near Napanoch. The formation is, as usual, a
light-colored, relatively pure limestone, with occasional lenses
and irregular layers of flint. It yields an excellent lime and
would furnish fine building stone in localities where there is a
sufficient thickness of beds free from chert. A mile northwest
of Pine Bush, on Mombaccus creek, the contact of the Esopus
shales and the Onondaga limestones is exposed. The upper

PLATE 19.

Awosting Falls of the Peterkill near Lake Minnewaska.

U of M

U of M

beds of the former are dark quartzitic sandstones, which give rise to a falls at this point. The basal portions of the limestone do not contain the thick beds of passage which exist further north, but it gives place very abruptly to the sandstones. About Wawarsing there are a number of exposures of several formations. Along the turnpike a mile east of the village there is an outcrop of the lower beds of the Esopus formation. They are black slates, separating along cleavage planes dipping steeply to the eastward. Their bedding is obscured by this cleavage, but it may be seen in some portions of the exposure dipping steeply to the westward. On the east side of the road the Oriskany formation is exposed in a low knoll; it is a silicious limestone ten to fifteen feet thick, dipping west-northwest thirty-five degrees. At the road forks the Onondaga limestone appears and is quarried and burnt at this point. Forty feet of this formation are exposed in this quarry, but there are more beds of it under the drift on either side. It is again seen at Napanoch in a quarry out in the meadow east of the turnpike. Here it originally came to the surface in a small knoll, and it is said that there are several similar small showings in the neighborhood. There are sixty feet of beds exposed in the quarry, dipping west-northwest forty-five degrees. Between Napanoch and Homowack there are no natural exposures of the Helderberg formation or of the immediately overlying rocks. It is stated that in the excavation for the canal, limestone was found near Homowack, and it is probably the Pentamerus bed, for the Shawangunk grits are exposed a short distance east. All the beds dip very steeply to the westward in this portion of the valley, and the Hamilton shales extend, together with the underlying formation, out under the lowlands east of the turnpike. The high hills rising to the westward are of the hard flaggy beds of the middle and upper Hamilton group which constitute a range lying between the Sandburg-Rondout valley and the Catskill mountains. This range is cut across by the Beerkill, Rondoutkill, Vernovy creek, Mombaccus creek and Metacahonts creek which flow through deep and rocky gorges. The beds are gray sandstones and flags with black shale intercalations and they are nearly everywhere exposed in the hill slopes and along

46

the streams. They dip steeply to the west-northwest about Ellenville and Napanoch, but this dip gradually decreases both to the north and to the west.

At Honk falls there is a fine exhibition of the steep dipping flaggy beds and this feature is shown in plate 20.

The dip at this locality is about forty-five degrees, a mile and a half west it is thirty degrees, and in the upper flag series, two and a half miles above the falls, it has decreased to ten degrees; at Lackawack it is not over three degrees.

THE CATSKILL MOUNTAIN REGION.

The Catskill mountains consist of a great thickness of sand-stones and shales, dipping gently to the westward. These members comprise the greater part of the upper flag formation, overlaid by the red conglomeratic sandstones which con-stitute the higher portions of the Slide mountain range and extend westward over the high ridges between the west branch of the Neversink and the Delaware county line. There are also on the very high summits of the Slide moun-tain range the light-colored, conglomeratic sandstones. In the mountains north of Esopus creek the conglomeratic members are not represented, although there are occasionally intercalated, at somewhat lower horizons, thin streaks of a conglomeratic character. The idea which has so long prevailed that the higher peaks of the Catskills are capped by remnants of a great sheet of conglomerate is erroneous, at least in the Ulster county region, for the conglomerates are in streaks and at sev-eral different horizons. The stratigraphy of the Catskill region is not uniform throughout and there are variations in the char-acters of the beds in different districts. The greater part of the lower series contains flagstone beds of great extent which have been quarried at a number of localities along Esopus creek and its branches and along the eastern front of the mountains.

The flags occur at various horizons, but the beds do not appear to be constant in character throughout. It is exceedingly difficult to trace them for any great distance, owing to talus on the slopes. The intercalated red shales occur in greatest force in the lower members, where they are numerous and thick. . They are not continuous beds but give place to flags, in some cases very

PLATE 20.

Honk?Falls, near Napanoch, N. Y. Over_inclined Beds of the Lower Flag Series. Looking North.

abruptly. The red shales occur in greatest amount to the northward and in lower members. Southward they become unimportant features of the stratigraphy, but there are several beds conspicuous in the lower members and others are contained at long intervals above. To the northward in the Overlook mountain region, they occur in frequent succession from the base of the mountains far up the slopes. Along the Esopus valley the red shales often occur in the lower members, but they are rare above. In the high region in the western part of the county, the formations are piled up to a thickness, which is not far from 4000 feet. Owing to frequent variation in the amount of dip, estimates of thickness for wide areas cannot be made with any degree of accuracy without elaborate measurements, and these I had not the time to make. A section through Slide mountain and adjoining ranges is given in the left end in figure 1, and this is typical for the higher bank of the southern Catskills.

The upper flag series in this portion of the region consists of thin to thick-bedded sandstones of moderately coarse grain, from brownish-gray to greenish-gray in color, sometimes reddish, with occasional intercalations of red shale which were not well exposed in the outcrops that I saw. This series grades above into coarser, thicker-bedded red sandstones containing quartz pebbles disseminated and in streaks of varying thickness. The rock cannot be considered a conglomerate except in some cases locally, where the conglomeratic portion attains a thickness of two or three feet and the pebbles are relatively close together. This, however, is rarely the case and such beds soon give place laterally to members characterized by a predominance of finer-grained material. The thickness of the series in Slide mountain is 1375 feet, but it thickens considerable to the westward of Hardenburgh township, where it is not less than 1500 feet. It constitutes the upper part of the Wittemburgh range and extends nearly to the edge of the county in the ridge between the upper Rondout and the east branch of the Neversink. Its western extension was not carefully studied, but the same characters appear to persist into Delaware county. These red beds are cut through by the Neversink and its branches, by the headwaters of Big Indian creek, and their divides, by Dry brook, Mill brook and the Beaverkill and are cut off by Rondout and Esopus creeks, beyond which they do not appear.

The white conglomeratic beds are separated from the underlying members by thin streaks of red shale, but this may be only a local feature.   On Slide mountain the beds consist of gray, buff and greenish-buff, coarse sandstone, with scattered pebbles and streaks of pebbles, which attain a thickness of 350 feet in the higher summit of the mountain.   There is a small 'cap of the formation on Mount Cornell, also on Wittemburgh and apparently also on Table mountain, Panther mountain and Peak-o-Moose.   It was thought that the western dip should carry this formation down to Double Top and Graham mountains, but these exhibit only the red conglomeratic beds at their summits.   It is, however, possible that the white beds are only a local phase of the eastern extension of the red deposits.

In the northern Catskills, in Woodstock township, particularly on Overlook mountain the Upper Flag series is extensively exposed. Ascending from Woodstock village to Overlook mountain there are alternations of red shales and gray or greenish-gray flags all the way to the top.   At an elevation of about 300 feet above Woodstock there is a particularly heavy bed of red shales which has a thickness of forty feet, and there are other thick beds near the summit.   The summit is a cap of hard, gray, flaggy sandstone twenty-five feet thick, lying on twenty-five feet of red shales. Along the road which passes just northward there are some alternations of underlying gray sandstones with thin streaks of red shales.   At one point north of the hotel about two hundred feet below the summit, there are thin streaks of quartz-conglomerate, of quartz and quartzitic pebbles in a gray sandstone matrix and again at a point 500 feet below this horizon several thin conglomeratic streaks are exposed on the southwest slope.

SOUTHEASTERN TOWNSHIPS.

The region extending from the eastern face of the Shawangunk mountains to the Hudson river is occupied by the Hudson river formation.   The greater part of the area is underlaid by slates and shales, but to the eastward in the high ridges extending from near Marlborough to Rondout there are sandstones and grits occupying a considerable area.   Much of the slate region is gently undulating with many low ridges of drift, and it is traversed by the wide valleys of the Wallkill and Swartkill,

PLATE 21.

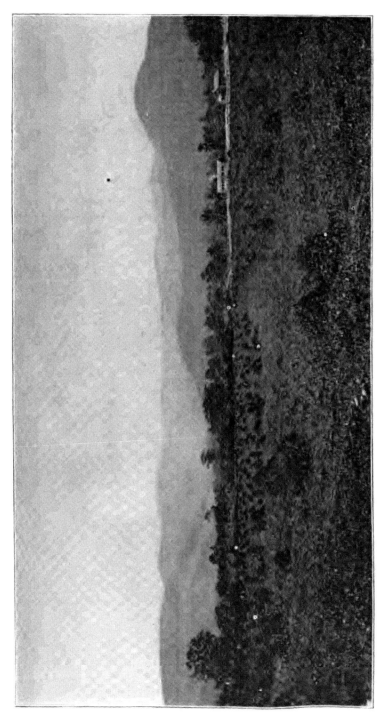

WITTEMBERG RANGE, SOUTHERN CATSKILLS, LOOKING WEST FROM WEST SHOKAN.

which are covered by alluvium. Slate outcrops are frequent, but the finest exposures are in the slopes of the Shawangunk mountain, along the Wallkill and in the bank of the Hudson river.

The predominant material is a brown-gray to black, moderately hard, fissile slate, often with marked cleavage and obscure bedding. There are many local intercalations of fine-grained sandstones, in greater part of dark color. At Rifton glen the Wallkill cuts deeply into the formation, and there are several extensive exposures in the banks. The beds are mainly horizontal, massively-bedded, fine-grained sandstones, with thin intercalations of shales. They are considerably broken below the falls, owing to local faults of small amount, and they are also considerably arched. Fossils occur at this point, comprising a number of distinctive Hudson river species. Near Eddyville the slates and sandstones are extensively exposed in the banks of Rondout creek, overlaid to the northward by the Salina and lower Helderberg formations. At Eddyville the slates are greatly contorted, and there is a fine exposure of these contortions in the creek banks. Along the eastern flanks of the Shawangunk mountain the Hudson river beds are soft shales, and these also, as already mentioned, are conspicuous in the eroded areas within the mountain, notably north of Lake Mohonk, at the southern end of Dickebar mountain; in the high hills of Mount Meenahga and in the gullies on the west slope of the mountain near Ellenville and Napanoch. In the vicinity of the Shawangunk mountain the slates dip northwest, with slight unconformity to the overlying Shawangunk grit, as already explained, but to the eastward the dip is to the southeast over a wide area extending to and beyond the Walkill river. The angles vary from thirty degrees to vertical, but from fifty degrees to seventy degrees are most frequent. The structure of the slates in the Walkill valley was not worked out, owing to the lack of definite stratigraphy and the absence of continuous outcrops along cross-section lines. Marlborough mountain and its northern continuations through Lloyd and Esopus townships are a series of high, narrow parallel ridges, consisting of hard, dark-gray, flaggy sandstones of moderately coarse grain. The beds stand nearly vertical and their structure is not clear. There

are apparently several distinct series of beds of these coarse
sandstones, separated by slates and sandy shales of moderate
thickness. The section east of Highland station is given in the
following figure :

FIG. 16. — Section through the northern end of Marlborough mountain from Clintondale
station to Highland station. Looking north.

The intermediate slate in the valley of Black creek was found
to be abundantly fossiliferous with a Hudson river fauna. No
fossils were found in the sandstones. A characteristic feature of
these sandstones is the occurrence of disseminated pebbles and
conglomeratic streaks of lighter-colored sandstones, of blue-gray
limestones of calciferous aspect and angular fragments of hard,
dark slates. No fossils were found in this conglomeratic material
but no extended search was made for them. The conglomeratic
streaks occur at several horizons apparently, but they are at a
considerable distance from the adjoining slates. These coarse-
grained members give place in part to finer-grained quartzitic
beds at some localities especially in the ridges north of West
Park station. They are best exposed in the deep cut of the West
Shore railroad between West Park and Esopus, where there are
seen massively-bedded, red quartzites standing nearly vertical or
dipping steeply to the southwest. Near Black creek, a few yards
from the railroad, these beds were quarried for abutments for
the railroad bridge, and although very hard and difficult to work
they afford an excellent material for such purposes. The high
ridges of hard beds extend west from Esopus nearly to the Rondout
creek, but are crossed by a relatively low depression at Ulster
park. To the eastward of Marlborough mountain and its
northern extensions there is a belt of slates similar to those of the
Wallkill and Swartkill valleys, but containing many intercalated
fine-grained sandstones which extend to the Hudson river.
The beds are finely exposed in the river banks, partly in the
many cuts of the West Shore railway. The slates in these cuts
are mainly gray, highly cleaved and steeply dipping. To the

south of New Paltz landing the cuts are particularly deep and exhibit a great variety of structural features in gray slates. Near the landing the dips are to the westward, forming a synclinal between the river and the high ridges of coarse rock westward. To the northward, part of this synclinal extends to the river and is exposed in the railroad cuts. The rocks involved are gray sandy shales and gray, flaggy, fine-grained sandstones. The shales are abruptly terminated south of Marlborough by a fault which brings up the Wappinger limestones.

The limestones occupy a small area in the extreme southeastern corner of the county. They are exposed in cliffs and railroad cuts extending continuously along the river bank to the Orange county line. They extend westward in rolling hills of typical limestone character, with many scattered outcrops. The dips are to the westward throughout, at an angle of ten degrees along the railroad and somewhat more in the hills west. In the vicinity of the fault there is considerable local disturbance, mainly fracturing. The relations of this fault are quite clearly exposed in the river bank, and in the following figure a sketch is given of the principal features.

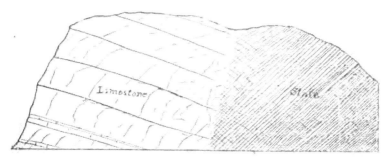

FIG. 17.—Section of fault one-half mile south of Marlborough station, on the Hudson river. Looking west. Based on a photograph.

The fault extends to the southwest and then west-southwest and passes out of the county. Its course inland is marked by an abrupt break between the rounded hills of slate and the knobby surface of limestone.

The limestone has been quarried to some extent, and in a quarry a short way above the railroad some of its upper members are well exposed.

As the stratigraphic relations of the limestones to the adjacent slates is not known the amount of the fault could not be determined. It crosses the Hudson northeastward, where it has been studied by Dwight.[*]

PLEISTOCENE GEOLOGY.

The Pleistocene formations consist of glacial drift of various kinds, alluvial accumulations and stratified clays and sands. I have not made a special examination of these formations and have but little to offer regarding them. The region has been extensively glaciated, and in some localities the products of glaciation are quite conspicuous. These are masses of drift, in greater part consisting of thin, irregular sheets extended over wide areas, and glacial striæ, scoring and polishing preserved on the surface of the harder rocks. The Shawangunk mountain presents the clearest evidences of this glaciation, which is conspicuous over nearly its entire area. This feature has been referred to by a number of observers, and Julien[†] has recorded the direction and nature of the striation at many points as follows:

"In the Sam's point region they are northeast and southwest, varying a few degrees on either side. Those trending south twenty-nine degrees west are most abundant, and there were fifteen to a foot, mostly about one-sixteenth of an inch deep. A few one-quarter of an inch in depth trended south seventy-five degrees west and south eighty-six degrees west. In following a long scratch southward there seemed to be a tendency to curve more and more toward a point nearer the west. In the vicinity of Lake Mohonk south ten degrees west was the direction observed at many points on the northwestern side of the mountain, and south forty degrees east on the southeastern side, and south eighteen degrees east on "Sky Top" at the summit of Paltz point; on the road to Alligerville south forty degrees east on the northwestern slope of the mountain. At Lake Minnewaska the direction is given as south ten degrees west."

It is suggested by Julien that the southeasterly direction on "Sky Top" may record the direction of the older and thicker glacial stream, while the others are due to local variations in

---

* Am. Jour. Science, III, vol. 81, pp. 125–183; one plate, 1886.

† New York Acad. Science, Trans., vol. 8, pp. 22–29.

PLATE 22.

Champlain Clays lying against the Old Shore-line of Helderberg Limestones in Brickyards along the Hudson River, One Mile North of Rondout, N. Y.
Looking Northwest.

depressions. Polishing is a very conspicuous feature on the mountain. The surfaces are frequently almost glassy, particularly on the higher portions of the western slopes where there are wide areas of polished surfaces. This may be due in part to local erosion and ice action. In the flag and Catskill regions the scoring and striation is frequently seen. The direction is mainly north-northeast to south-southwest, but is very variable within limits of a few degrees, particularly in the lower altitudes.

The alluvial deposits of Ulster county comprise sands, gravels and boulders along the streams and peat and marl deposits in some of the adjacent lowlands. The upper valleys of Esopus and Rondout creeks contain a large amount of relatively recent gravels and boulders more or less intermixed with sands, and nearly all the small stream depressions contain similar deposits at intervals. There are along the wider valleys of the eastern part of the county extensive deposits of stratified clays and sands and in the lowest terraces greater or less accumulations of recent alluviums. The clays and sands constitute a terrace of varying width bordering the Hudson river to below Port Ewen and extending up the Rondout creek by Ellenville, up the Wallkill to Orange county and a long distance up Esopus creek. They are the products of a submergence at the close of the glacial epoch, which is known as the Champlain period. During this submergence the waters of the Hudson extended over the area now occupied by the deposits, which have since been elevated and cut into by the present drainage.

These deposits extend up to an altitude averaging about 250 feet to the westward and to considerably less along the Hudson. They consist normally of a clay deposit below overlaid to a greater or less thickness by sand. At points where the streams entered the submerged area at the time of the deposition of these deposits there are also found delta deposits of coarser materials. The clays lie on thin, irregular masses of glacial sands and gravels or on glaciated surfaces of rocks. Mr. Heinrich Ries * has recently published a preliminary account of these

---

* The Quaternary deposits of the Hudson River valley between Croton and Albany, with notes
on the brick clays and the manufacture of brick. 10th annual report, State Geologist, 1890.
110-158. Albany, 1891.

deposits in the Hudson valley, and from this work the following observations are taken:

From Glasco to Rondout the terrace, which is perhaps one-eighth of a mile broad at Glasco, narrows as it nears Rondout and has an average height of 150 feet. The clays, so far as could be ascertained, lie on the upturned edges of the shale. In the Van Dusen yard at Glasco the clay is in places "as much as seventy feet thick and is mostly blue, with several feet of loams on top." The clay lies on a ridge of shale which rises steeply from the shore for some sixty feet. "At the Washburn yards the blue clay has a thickness of 132 feet, with four feet of yellow clay and six to eight feet of fine sand above. It lies on shale at an altitude of eight feet above the river." At the rear of A. S. Staple's yard (two miles north of Rondout) there is an exposure of "hardpan" underlying the clay. The overlying material at this locality consists of sand and gravel, in some cases stratified and sometimes cross-bedded. The sand in some spots is ten to fifteen feet thick and fine enough to be blown by the wind. At Hutton's yard (near by) the blue clay is exposed from eight feet above tide to 110 feet; above this there is about ten feet of yellow and over this about fifteen feet of sand.

At Port Ewen the clay is mostly blue, resting on a mass of hardpan and in a few places on the glaciated rock surface. The clay seems to lie as a deposit eighteen to twenty feet thick on the hardpan and is in turn overlaid in many places by fine stratified sand. A point worthy of notice is the difference in level of fifty feet between the terrace at Port Ewen and that at Glasco. This may be due to the fact that when sediment is deposited in a basin its upper surface will be higher at the edge of the basin than in the center. The quaternary formation broadens out at Port Ewen toward the west and Port Ewen would be on a point of the basin's edge, while Glasco is near the center. At Port Ewen the terrace is 207 feet above the river, but it must be fully 225 feet at the base of Hussey mountain, which was probably an island in the estuary.

The thickness of the clay between Glasco and Rondout varies considerably, amounting to 120 feet in places, and in others not over twenty feet. This is owing to the great irregularity of the underlying rock surface.

PLATE 28.

TYPICAL FLAG OR BLUE STONE QUARRY, QUARRYVILLE, N. Y. LOOKING NORTH.

The narrowest part in the terrace is a mile north of Rondout, where its width is not over 200 yards. In the yards of Terry Brothers the clay has been quarried back to the old shore line of the deposits, which is a high overhangi··g cliff of Helderberg limestone. The relations at this locality are shown in plate 22.

This high, steep shore extends for some distance in this region, but lies farther back from the river elsewhere.

In the Walkill, Rondout and Esopus valleys the Champlain deposits are thick and extensive. East of Rosendale there is a wide sand plain of the upper member extending from the Rondout creek to the Walkill. In the Rondout valley above High Falls the clay deposits are very thick and they rise in high terraces along the turnpike and eastward. At Pine Bush the sand member is conspicuous, constituting a high, narrow ridge trending eastward and separating the Mombaccus and Rondout creeks. The lower portion of this ridge is clay apparently, which extends to its base.

It is thought that the low divides of the Catskill are due to glacial action, mainly to the diversion of streams by ice dams.

Fig. 18 — Wagonwheel gap from Sampsonville. Looking north.

Possibly they were in part pre-existent as part of an early base level system, but this possibility has not yet been carefully considered. They are largely in the direction of the ice movement,

notably Stony clove, Mink hollow, Peak-o-Moose clove and Big
Indian divide. One of the most remarkable of these features is
in the southern Catskills. It is a gap across the long eastern
spur of "High Point" mountain. It is known as Wagonwheel
gap and is a conspicuous feature in the region. Its character
is shown in the preceding figure.

The gap is cut across the spur very much after the manner of
a high railroad cut, but its bottom slopes from a divide near its
center. Its depth is about 200 feet. It is, I believe, a product
of glacial times and was cut by Esopus creek while the valley
was dammed by ice in the vicinity of Shokan. I have not studied
the locality with care, and this should be regarded only as a
suggestion.

Respectfully yours.

N. H. DARTON.

CPSIA information can be obtained at www.ICGtesting.com
Printed in the USA
BVOW031927220112

281128BV00005B/74/P

9 781120 681164